ENOUGH ALREADY
Seven Yoga-Inspired Steps to Calm Amid Chaos

ELAINE JACKSON

Enough Already
© 2020 by Elaine Jackson
All Rights Reserved.
Cover design by Castelane.

Published in the United States of America.

No part of this book may be reproduced or transmitted in any form or by any means electronic or mechanical, including photocopying, recording, or by an information storage and retrieval system without written permission of the author and publisher.

Although every precaution has been taken to verify the accuracy of the information contained herein, the author and publisher assume no responsibility for any errors or omissions. No liability is assumed for damages that may result from the use of the information contained within.

ISBN 13: 978-1-7772620-0-6

Contents

Foreword	9
Introduction	11
A Note on the Languages of Yoga and Buddhism	15
Part One: Concentration	**17**
Samyama: The Inward Journey	19
Pratyahara and the Wisdom of the Turtle	25
Bonding or Branding?: Social Media and the Attention Economy	29
We're All Addicted to Something	34
Part Two: Mindfulness	**37**
The Tidal Pull Toward Awakening	39
Simple But Not Easy	41
A Time and A Place — Some Cautionary Notes	44
Motivation to Meditate (When You Don't Feel Like It)	47
The Art of Intimate Surveillance	50
Form Versus Substance	53
Tapas: The Space Where Change Can Happen	57
Mindful Insomnia	60
The Princess and the Bodhi Seed	64
Part Three: Investigation	**69**
Impermanence and the Fear of Life	71
Everybody Hurts, Sometimes	74
Becoming More Flexible About Self-hood	80
Feeling Groovy: Habit Patterns and Samskaras	84
Hungry Ghosts	87
How Our Words Shape Who We Are	89
What's Going on with My Energy?: The Three Gunas	91
Echoes of Narcissus	94
The Secret Power of the Stories We Tell	98
Hearing Impaired	102
And Out of the Darkness Came the Light	106

Part Four: Virya: What Do I Stand For? — 109
    Karma and Consequences: We Are What We Do — 111
    Yoga Ethics: The Yamas and the Niyamas — 115
    First, Do No Harm: Ahimsa — 119
    Aparigraha and Generosity — 123
    Honesty — It's Complicated — 126
    Not Stealing Is Harder Than You'd Think — 129
    The Wise Tending of Sexual Energy — 131
    Churning the Ocean: How to Navigate Difficult Emotions — 137
    A Tool for Working with Self-Judgment — 140
    Water Is Precious — 144
    Appropriate Anger — 147
    Goldilocks Yoga — 150
    Embodying the Warrior — 152

Part Five: Joy — 155
    A Bright Light in a Dark Time — 157
    Awe and Samadhi — 159
    Compassion Makes Us Happier — 162
    "Wild Thing, You Make My Heart Sing" — 165
    Grace After Meals — 168
    The Wisdom of No Advice: Memories of an Afternoon in Bed — 170

Part Six: Relaxation — 173
    The Ways We Run Away: Relaxing Versus Avoiding — 176
    Losing One's Head — 179
    The King, the Prince, and the Sands of Time — 181
    Having Enough: Cultivating Contentment — 185
    A Series of Successive Approximations — 187
    The Ugly Duckling — 190
    Just Breathe — 193
    Beauty, Health, and Wabi-sabi — 196
    Beginner's Mind — 198
    Looking Through a Longer Lens — 200

Part Seven: Equanimity — 203
    A Trinity of Practices — 205
    "There's a Starman Waiting in the Sky" — 208

To Thine Own Self Be True	210
Be Kind to Yourself	214
Your Gifts Will Bring You Home	217
Coping with Grief	222
Samsara and Its Antidotes	225
Ten Characteristics of Resilient People	228
Mono No Aware	231
The Brahmaviharas	233
Equanimity Reprised	236
Wonder and the Source	239
Friendship	243
Awakened and Free	246
Notes	248
Glossary	255
Recommended Reading	258
Acknowledgments	260

For my parents, Maurice and Marie, who gave me everything they had to give and who are living proof that we never stop growing.

And for Dave, a bear of few words but with the biggest and most generous of hearts.

You practice with your whole heart, and slowly, slowly, the door begins to open from the other side.
— Michael Stone

Then would you read a sustaining book, such as would help and comfort a wedged bear in great tightness?
— A.A. Milne

Foreword

Dozens of blog notifications and newsletters land in my inbox every day, every week, every month. Most of them I throw into a file labeled "Read Later." If I accidentally deleted that "Read Later" file, I wouldn't miss it. It's a kind of intellectual or spiritual hoarding. Though I think I might learn something within them, I will never go back to most of them.

Out of those many, many emails I get, there are only two or three that I read without fail the moment they arrive. Elaine Jackson's JOY newsletter is one of them. And that is because I recognize myself in each one of her sentences: a recognition that happens through the lens she holds—a lens of wise compassion for our human foibles.

I am a psychotherapist, a student of Hakomi, a writer, and a facilitator of writing workshops. Elaine and I met through our mutual love of writing and deepened our friendship through discovering our shared values. It's my belief that one of the reasons Elaine invited me to write the foreword to *Enough Already* is that she'd read a blog post I wrote about choosing two words to have tattooed on my wrists—one on each. One of the two words was "enough." In that post I wrote about a momentary epiphany I had around doing the best we can, and accepting that that is enough.

It's something I've been wrestling with for a long time. How do we balance wanting to do more, be better, and fulfill our potential, with believing we are enough just as we are? An incredibly wise therapist once told me that our work as human beings is to learn to hold ourselves in warm regard in spite of our very human failings. This book is a guidebook for how to do that.

How do we challenge ourselves, gently, to become who we have the capacity to be, while holding ourselves without negative judgment and in loving presence when we struggle?

This beautiful book you're holding in your hand will be a compassionate and intelligent guide to finding skillful answers to those questions.

Gathered together here are many of the subjects that Elaine has mused on and struggled with in those missives, but now they are collected in a way where each one builds on what has come before. She also fills in pieces that are new, that expand topics that she touched on before but that left me hungry for more.

This book is an invitation to become awakened and free—it's an appeal to each of us to make the most of our "one wild and precious life," both for ourselves and for the collective good of our communities and our world.

Enough Already includes a series of strategies to let go of our limited ideas about self and to become much more spacious (which, for those of you who were holding that question, is the word on my other wrist).

The path described in this book includes a blueprint for how to let go of stories about "them and us," or about "me vs. the world." Ultimately, it offers us techniques for letting more love into our lives.

And more love in our lives is probably one of the few things that we can never have enough of.

Sue Reynolds,
September 2020

Introduction

One of the most difficult questions I was ever asked came from an athletic twenty-seven-year-old entomologist who was quickly and inexorably losing his mind to schizophrenia. We were sitting across from one another in a boxy, windowless assessment room. He pushed the forms we'd been filling out aside, gazed into my eyes and said, despondently, "If you were in my shoes, what would you do?"

He'd already attempted to kill himself twice, and had lost his girlfriend, his employment, and his home. I was an occupational therapist tasked with helping him find purpose and hope, and in answer to his question, I had nothing. Sure, I could assure him that things could get better, new drugs could become available, supports could be put in place—but those were "pat" answers he'd heard many times before. I'm sure those were the answers I gave him, but that day I felt their hollowness.

Inwardly I thought, "I'd probably want to kill myself too."

When I started my career I was full of idealism and theory, but as I came into contact day after day with real, complex, existential suffering, I quickly grasped that I didn't have tools to deal with it, either professionally or personally. Of course I did what I could: I listened, researched and asked for help from colleagues, but my empathy was dragging me down the ramp to burnout city. The tools I had were great for pragmatic issues (can't walk, let's get a wheelchair) but not for the suffering or the painful realities of permanent disability, dementia, or impending death. I soon recognized that I needed to improve my capacity to simply *be* with that suffering, without my delusions about fixing it.

Eventually I took up yoga to help deal with the stress. I'd dabbled with it in the eighties, but gave up because I lived in a dodgy neighborhood where

I got harassed by pimps and johns on my walk home from sessions. In the nineties I had a new address and found some great teachers. I studied in earnest, and ten years later completed my first teacher training. Near the end of that two-year period I met the teacher of yoga philosophy and Buddhism who radically changed my worldview, and my life—Michael Stone. I studied and worked with him for thirteen years, until his heartbreaking death in 2017. Michael was a soul-friend and mentor. He was brilliant, loving, at times challenging, imaginative, and funny. I could talk to him about *everything*, and I miss him terribly.

As I continued to work as a therapist, I decided also to pursue an abandoned dream of becoming a writer. In my late thirties I went back to university and completed a degree in creative writing and then an MA in English literature. My focus was still on finding meaning and happiness, and my master's thesis explored the utopian writings of Ursula K. Le Guin. I continued to study philosophy, Buddhism, and yoga throughout, juggling multiple jobs in a way that now, looking back, makes my head spin.

I've been studying and teaching yoga and mindfulness for more than fifteen years, and my fascination with the interconnectedness of body, mind, and spirit is as great as ever. But now, thanks to many talented teachers and friends, I feel the tools I have to manage suffering (mine and others) are more varied, practical, and suited to the task.

In the last few years I've written extensively about yoga and mindfulness. I'd always dreamed of re-casting these pieces into a larger, coherent whole. But it seemed that just as I set out to do so, the world grew radically weirder: extremist movements that horrified me, along with racist rants, toxic politics, bizarre fake news stories, a growing ecological crisis, and also, disappointingly, a commercialization of yoga that sometimes focused more on its benefits for reducing cellulite than its potential as a path to spiritual awakening.

Enough already.

The personal essays in this book were written primarily to assuage and clarify my own distress, my own questions, my own need to find peace and calm. As I write, we're facing the COVID-19 pandemic, which we already know will change everything in the years to come, in ways we can't yet imagine. Most yoga teachers, myself included, are only teaching a minuscule portion of what we'd like to be teaching in our weekly classes. This book is an opportunity for me take you, the reader, deeper.

I feel a sense of urgency now, to share these teachings with as many people as possible. In looking for a unifying structure, I came across a set of teachings from the Buddha known as The Seven Factors of Awakening. These seven stages—concentration, mindfulness, investigation, virya, relaxation, joy, and equanimity—represent a journey toward courage and calm, toward a life with more wisdom and less self-imposed suffering. Although I've described them in a structure that feels linear, these factors can be studied and pursued in any order. Each one feeds and supports the others.

Human beings have an enormous capacity for creativity, problem solving, love, and cooperation. We also have the capacity for destruction, greed, hatred, and delusion. We are creatures who manufacture meaning and who are free to make choices. But we're also mammals, dependent on nervous systems that when stressed, don't lead us to good decisions. If we want to manage effectively the multiplicity of crises we're facing, we've got to get a handle on our own capacity to deal. We have to look after our bodies, minds, and spirits, and find a way to tone down our arousal levels. We may care deeply about what's happening in the world, care deeply about the welfare of all beings, but first we must be able to steady and soothe ourselves. Not in the usual way we think about self-care—or *self*, or *care*, for that matter (i.e., the gym, the diet, the vitamin supplements, the vacations) but rather by cultivating skills for the body and mind that can help us to overcome our pain and delusions—personally and societally.

The teachings in *Enough Already* call into question the very idea of selfhood, and how we differentiate between what is real to our experience and what is imposed or driven by larger forces. Caring for the self can be viewed as a conscious, deliberate strategy to transform passivity to creativity; to live our lives, as limited as they might be by our circumstances, with passion, imagination, and ferocious love.

The "Practice & Reflect" sections at the end of each chapter provide suggestions for readers who would like to dive deeper. I've included some embodied practices as well as questions for you to consider and/or write about. I'd recommend using a journal so that you can keep your responses in one place. These are open-ended exercises without right or wrong answers, and they're not designed to tell you what to do. Instead, they're meant to help you translate these ideas into more personalized insights or actions, based on your unique circumstances and experiences.

I hope this book will give you new ways of thinking about yoga, mindfulness, and your life. Together let's move, as the title says, toward calm amid chaos.

Elaine Jackson
April 2020

A Note on the Languages of Yoga and Buddhism

Sanskrit is the original language of Yoga, and like all languages it is a vast and complex subject to study. The written form is a script called Devanāgāri, and the translation of these symbols into English sounds is an inexact science.

Some translators, for example, will spell *santosha* with an "n" and others will spell it *samtosha* with an "m," because apparently the pronunciation of the Sanskrit consonant falls somewhere between the two. To further complicate matters, there are regional differences in pronunciation, just as there are different accents in English.

The Buddha's teachings were recorded in a language called Pali, which was based on Sanskrit but was a "street" language that ordinary people could speak. Analogous to Latin, Sanskrit was the language of priests and scholars. Thus, we see the word *dharma* in yoga texts and *dhamma* in Buddhist texts, but they have the same meaning.

For those who are interested, vast amounts of information are available online. One excellent source is lexilogos.com/english/sanskrit_dictionary.htm.

For the quickest route to pronouncing a Sanskrit or Pali word, I recommend typing "how do I pronounce ____" into your search engine.

I have not been faithful to the Sanskrit diacritical marks (which, like accents, provide guidance about pronunciation) in this text. I chose to omit them rather than spend many hours in the black hole of "special characters" and conflicting dictionaries. To the purists out there, I apologize.

Part One: Concentration

In the wholeheartedness of concentration world and self begin to cohere. With that state comes an enlarging: of what may be known, what may be felt, what may be done.
— Jane Hirshfield

The first step on our journey together has to do with the ability to concentrate. I say this as the owner of a mind that is as clear and focused as a hoarder's garage. On many occasions I've been in the middle of making dinner when I remember an email I was supposed to answer, and then once online I get distracted by an e-newsletter or Facebook post, and then thirty minutes later go back to making dinner and realize that I don't actually have time to finish making it, because I have an appointment to get to or a class to teach. And then as I'm eating my toast over the sink, I'm full of self-recrimination, and that's usually when I put the teapot in the fridge and go chasing off in search of my car keys. If this sounds familiar, at least know that misery loves company. Thanks to a culture that increasingly revolves around technology, we all experience some level of attention-fail. And now we have the options of losing focus on multiple platforms and with more people than ever.

Without focus and the ability to sustain our attention, we never get anything done. We end up half-assing our way through life, eating takeout because the meal-planning and grocery shopping got bumped off the list. We feel short of time, rushed, breathless—all the time. We make poor decisions, because we're not present enough to fully process information. We usually get the tasks done that hinge on accountability to others—the report for the boss, or the essay for school—but our own dreams and creative yearnings get relegated to the "Later" file. And all of this distraction has momentum. We get so used to feeling this way that when asked to stop, we get uncomfortable. Our fingers itch for the screen of our smartphones. We have become addicted to constant input, and our attention gets snapped up by whatever is the most sparkly, novel, or shocking. But we never actually digest anything. We're in a state of constant overload.

Concentration is important not only for doing, but also for being. There's nothing quite so frustrating as trying to have a conversation with someone who clearly is only half listening. Yep. Even relationships require concentration.

The cultivation of concentration is an important aspect of yoga and mindfulness, but it's also just a basic life skill with which we're all losing touch. We need concentration to make good decisions, control impulses, complete complex tasks, and also, to gain insight into our habits and behaviors. Concentration makes our minds stronger and wiser.

Practice & Reflect

Journal:

- Write down your three favorite distractions.
- How could you put some boundaries around them?

Practice:

- Take a moment to connect with your natural breathing.
- Once you are fully aware of it, begin to count, silently, on the inhale and exhale.
- Inhale one, two, three, and then exhale one, two, three.
- Repeat twelve times.[1]

Samyama: The Inward Journey

*If you can't find the truth right where you are,
where else do you expect to find it?*
— Dōgen

The traditional path of yoga, as outlined in Patanjali's Yoga Sutras (a text published around 200 B.C.E.), has eight limbs, which when practiced together lead toward the ideal outcome, which is to reunite the small, everyday self with the universal, timeless, all-encompassing self (sometimes described as God, or Nature, or the Universe, or Enlightenment). As those of us who've taught yoga for a long time readily admit, those Instagram posts showing beautiful people in mind-blowing postures are the "loss leader" we're hoping will entice you into the store. Yoga is fundamentally a spiritual practice, and a psychological one. The side benefits include better posture and more pliant hamstrings. What's not to love?

Concentration is both one of the limbs of the eight-part model and an important skill that is developed at every stage. The yoga journey begins with redefining our relationship with the world "outside" and then progresses gradually toward our interior experience. As we complete the journey, the differentiation between outside and inside itself slips away (Illustration on page 20).

The path begins with guidelines regarding how we behave toward others (the yamas) and how we care for ourselves (the niyamas). The next two stages are asana (postures and movement) and pranayama (becoming intimate with the breath and learning to free it).

The first four steps are focused outward, toward the senses and the pragmatic functions of the mind. The ethics (yamas and niyamas) help us negotiate being in relationships, and the asanas help us manage and explore our physical embodiment. Pranayama gives us a tool to work with our nervous system (by way of our respiratory system). The fifth step, pratyahara, is the ability to unhook the senses from external stimuli, which allows us to transition between our everyday outer world and the inner world of our consciousness.

THE YOGA JOURNEY

The last three steps on the yoga path are collectively called samyama (fusion), or antara yoga, which means "inward journey." The first of these three is called *dharana*, and is sometimes translated as "concentration." The second is called *dhyana*, or "meditation," and the last is *samadhi*, which means "union" or "integration."

Meditation is the practice, or "form," that we use to build the skills needed for our inward journey. Once we can disconnect from distractions and steady our attention, we can learn to focus on one thing. Some people use a mantra or sound, others a visual drawing, or yantra, or still others use a sensation in the body. By far the most common object to use is the breath (you can't forget it at home, and you can find it anywhere and at any time). No breath, no need to worry about attention.

Language for working with consciousness can be a stumbling ground; for example, is focus different from concentration? Depending on the yoga lineage or even the yoga teacher, we can use different terms to describe similar experiences. Nischala Devi is reluctant to equate dharana with concentration, because we often associate concentration with effort and a "tightening" of the body and mind. She believes dharana is a gentle and relaxed state, and therefore prefers to call it "contemplation" or "reflection."[2] Whether concentration is always relaxed is up for debate, because the situation it happens in will have an effect. As neurological science becomes ever more advanced, I can imagine a time when we might be able to refine or differentiate these mind states with brain scans—but until then, yogis describe these experiences with the tools they have at hand: body, language, and imagination (such as sacred texts, tales of gods and goddesses, mudras, or symbols).

Explore States of Consciousness

Before going deeper into dharana, let's touch on the next two stages: dhyana and samadhi. Dhyana is often translated as "meditation," or "mindfulness," and is described as the ability to stay focused for a prolonged period. Samadhi is more of a transcendent state, where the mind is so concentrated that it fuses with either the object of meditation, or the Divine (if that language speaks to you). In samadhi, the sense of ego-self in isolation drops away completely.

What is the difference between dharana and dhyana? In B.K.S. Iyengar's *Light on Pranayama*, he explains that the root of *dharana*, *dhr*, means "to hold," or "concentration." Dharana, he says, is like a lamp with a shade on it; it only illuminates a small area. Whereas when the cover is removed, it can light up the whole room. The more open and diffuse light compares to dhyana, which he calls the "expansion of consciousness."[3] Some teachers point out that dhyana is what happens when we're absorbed in a subject or task that interests us deeply.

Perhaps the easiest way to think about the inward journey is to imagine a spectrum with distraction or inattention at the far end and complete absorption (samadhi) at the other. I like to use as an example the analogy of learning a new skill. Imagine you are learning to skate for the first time. Initially, you fall down repeatedly, and it takes a lot of mental exertion and concentration (dharana) to stay upright. With time and practice you gain enough skill to both stay on your feet and navigate around cracks in the ice or fellow skaters without losing your balance. You may fatigue quickly, but you gradually improve your endurance. This state would be analogous to sustained concentration or meditation (dhyana). Eventually, with practice and gumption, you become so comfortable and skilled that you fall in love with skating. Once you're out on the rink you become enchanted with sensations (muscles moving, crisp, fresh air, the sun sparkling on the snow) and experience joy. The thought of a "me" doing a thing (skating) dissolves: there's just a fusion of body, mind, and object (which in this case is an activity). There's a feeling that time has stopped, the babbling inner voice has gone quiet, and nothing exists beyond this delight. You may stay in this state for a few seconds or a few minutes until something brings you back to your surroundings. Then you remember that you've got an appointment to get to, and you return to your everyday mind.

Train the Attention

When it comes to yoga and meditation, dharana is a practice of strengthening our capacity to pay attention, even when the object is not perceived as interesting. In our concentration training, the attention may "fall off" fairly frequently, and the work is to keep starting over, without becoming frustrated and without being unkind to oneself. As we get better at it, dharana naturally segues into dhyana, a mind state where the attention stays tethered to its object even as the mind continues its cinematic and eclectic putzing away.

All these labels, categories and descriptions are conceptual. They don't necessarily happen in the order or the way they are described here or exist in a way that we can differentiate with objective measurements. We can say that meditative practices do affect brain waves, but we can't say at this point that we're in one state or another based on what we're seeing on an MRI.

For those with a tendency to overthink things, it's important not to get sidetracked by trying to make your experiences fit the model. Some of the best meditators I know don't even actually meditate. They are those rare people who drop into "flow" states and remain focused with ease—a gift that has less to do with intellect or willpower than with loving whatever they're doing.

The most important takeaway? There's plenty to explore when it comes to human consciousness, and these ancient practices can function as maps. But the map and the territory are not the same thing. As the Zen teaching points out, we mustn't mistake the finger pointing at the moon for the moon itself. Also, as yoga teacher Matt Remski says, meditation is what happens in the mind-body in response to the instructions given. In other words, you can trust in your own feelings and your own experience.[4]

We can wander around without maps, or we can use them for orientation. Either way, we're going on a trip.

Practice & Reflect

> Note: Anytime you are using your phone timer, for any of these practice activities, it's a good idea to place it well out of reach once you've set it, so you won't be tempted to look at it.

Meditation Preparation:

You can easily create your own meditation space. The key is to build a place for habit, for ritual.

- Find a private corner, or a room, or even a spacious closet big enough for a cushion or chair, where you can be undisturbed and technology-free.
- Set up a cushion or a chair that you can leave there. If your space is tiny, be inventive; you may have to move your cushion under the bed when you're not using it. Make it cozy.
- Make it unique and personal: add a candle, a photo that inspires you, or something natural or beautiful from outside (a stone, a pine cone, a flower).

Meditation Practice:

- Set timer for five minutes.
- Sit on your meditation cushion or a chair.
- Take a moment to locate and feel the movement of your breath, in and out.
- Then, on your next exhale, say silently to yourself, "Ten."
- The following exhale will be nine, and then eight, and so on until you get down to one.
- When you reach one, start again at ten.
- If you get distracted and lose count, start again at ten.

Pratyahara and the Wisdom of the Turtle

We withdraw not to disappear, but to find another ground from which to see; a solid ground from which to step, and from which to speak again, in a different way, a clear, rested, embodied voice...
— David Whyte

I have a lot of warrior in me. I'm the type of person who gets outraged easily, and I get emotional when I witness acts of ignorance, injustice, or plain short-sightedness. I've had to work hard to balance this trait with more patience, empathy, and compassion. I also live in dread of hurting people—intentionally or otherwise. I have plenty of buttons that are easy to push. My teacher, Michael, explained that this is why the test of our yoga achievements is not about how long we can sit on a cushion, or how impressive our poses look, but rather how we conduct ourselves in our relationships.

But in every relationship, we have to know when to go deeper, and when to retreat. Sometimes, when we can't figure out a skillful way to behave or respond, we have to withdraw from stimuli that are toxic or painful to us, at least temporarily. In this light I've been pondering the limb of yoga called pratyahara.

A number of practices fall under the umbrella of pratyahara. *Prati* is a preposition meaning "against," and *ahara* means "anything we take into ourselves from the outside."[5] Sometimes the practice is described as being like a turtle withdrawing into its shell. Nothing in the outer world changes, but the practitioner is able to create a space that feels safe and steady.

Some yoga lineages practice pratyahara in a truly literal way—physically closing the eyes, and blocking the ears with the hands.[6] Some practice it with machismo, by meditating in a mosquito-infested forest and not reacting to the bites. (If you're interested, I have plenty of mosquitos in my backyard you can practice with.) But most, I think, treat it more organically, as a shift from noticing what is outside to paying attention to what is inside, from the external world to our own consciousness. When we lie down on the mat at the beginning of a class to "tune in" to the body, we are practicing a form of pratyahara.

There are at least four kinds:

- Control of sensory impressions is the first, and it can be understood to happen at both the intake stage and the processing stage. For example, we can control how much entertainment based on violence and gratuitous sex we take in. But we can also practice monitoring how we react to sensory stimuli, asking, "What am I finding enjoyable in this story about serial killers and violence?"
- Control of what we ingest, which would include limiting junk food and limiting toxic substances like drugs or alcohol. We could also include not using toxic substances on our skin or hair, or pesticides on our lawns (since they eventually end up ingested through our water or the food chain).
- Control of our associations (the people we let into our lives). Are we in relationships with people who are abusive, narcissistic. or excessively selfish; or people who bring out the worst in us; or people who lead us toward our addictions or triggers? Can we distance ourselves from these people?
- Control of our actions. Can we withdraw from situations where we are not making wise choices? Can we take a break so that we're not acting from anger, or impulsivity? Can we pause before we press "send" on that critical email?

On all these levels, pratyahara becomes a practice of discernment and self-awareness. And often it requires that we actively audit and manage where our time and attention goes. An example: other than morbid curiosity and titillation, my occasional binge-watching of *Forensic Files* does nothing to improve me or anything else in my world. Really, my time would be better spent reading or volunteering somewhere. Cognitive scientists have recognized that we have a limited amount of attentional bandwidth. The yogis understood that how we choose to make use of that resource matters to our overall well-being.

Many yoga teachers advise that it is better not to watch the news, because the senses and emotions become overwhelmed and lead to unskillful actions. I've always felt resistance to this, because burying our heads in the sand can lead to even worse outcomes—genocides being a case in point. I believe Edmund Burke's assertion that "Bad men need nothing more to compass their ends, than that good men should look on and do nothing." But lately I am seeing more wisdom in at least partially withdrawing my attention from the news. At least until I get a handle on how I'm going to respond to it. I haven't stopped paying attention, but I'm building some boundaries around when I watch it (never right before bed), the sources I follow (real journalism versus Facebook), and how long I spend doing it. My husband and I have subscribed to a paper (they desperately need the support), and I no longer consume news randomly online.

Pratyahara could be described as a practice of building boundaries around our attentional resources. Or think of it as being like leash-training a dog; it allows her to go out with you but keeps her safe from passing cars and other dangers. Practicing pratyahara means recognizing that what we take in has an effect on our outlook, our energy, and ultimately our capacity to create. I've realized that my time is better spent seeking out the people who are doing great things in the world and people who are focusing on finding solutions, versus the trolls on the internet who do nothing but sneer and criticize. Pratyahara puts us back in attentional control, so we can appreciate and tend to what is nourishing: like the cat purring on our lap, the sun shining in the window, and the people in our lives who bring us joy.

Practice & Reflect

Coming home to your shell:

- Place your dominant hand on your sternum, right over your heart.
- Then place your non-dominant hand on top of it.

- Feel the heaviness of your hands, the weight and the warmth of them.
- Imagine breathing into them.
- Close your eyes and stay in this position for ten to twenty breaths.

Child's Pose:

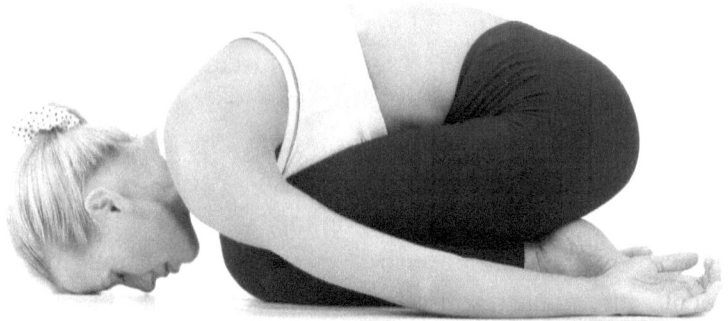

This is the preferred posture of introverts everywhere.

- If you don't suffer from knee pain, transition into the pose by kneeling on all fours, knees wide, toes together.
- Lower your sitting bones to your heels.
- Your head will rest on the floor (or on your stacked fists or a yoga block), and your arms will rest at your sides (see illustration).
- Stay for ten to twenty breaths.[7]

Bonding or Branding?: Social Media and the Attention Economy

> *Researchers in the new field of interruption science have found that it takes an average of twenty-five minutes to recover from a phone call. Yet such interruptions come every eleven minutes—which means we're never caught up with our lives.*
> — Pico Iyer

Not long ago, I was invited to a yoga teacher training to lead a workshop on breathing techniques. I asked the trainees to turn off their cell phones and sit in a circle while we practiced some beginner exercises together. The level of anxiety in the room was palpable. I tried to put them at ease: I asked them about what they were feeling, and guided them to take breaks as needed. My comments were met with silence. A few days later I called the host to debrief and mentioned feeling a lot of tension in the room. She explained that almost all of the students had anxiety disorders, and making eye contact with a stranger was really hard for them. They'd all felt intimidated when I asked for their undivided attention.

When I worked as an occupational therapist I was interested in "attention retraining," because attentional processes are often impaired by brain injuries. The ability to sustain attention on one task over a period of time is described as concentration, and it forms the foundation of many other brain functions—including learning and remembering. When attention is divided, such as when we're multitasking, although we *feel* we're accomplishing more, we're usually remembering less and making more errors. We also tend to become more impatient and irritable, because of the quantity of sensory stimuli we are asking our brains to process.

The generation of students in the room were digital natives: too young to remember a life without the internet, and used to being connected throughout all their waking hours. Too young to even question whether the constant barrage on their social feeds is beneficial to their lives. They have no experiential reference for comparison.

I have a tortured relationship with social media, because although I see its benefits, I believe it's altering our brains and our mental health. I love that I can connect with distant friends and relatives, especially in a situation like the 2020 pandemic. I love that I can be part of professional groups where I can ask questions and share ideas. I love that activists, innovators, and scientists can use social media to get important information to the public. But my fear is that on a psychological and spiritual level, social media is alienating us from our embodied experience and affecting our ability to form deep relationships.

The command "Pay attention" is more apt and more relevant the more we learn about neuroscience. Attention, like money, is a limited resource, and it's the pot of gold that marketers are scrambling to capture. Social media platforms generate revenue by selling our attention to businesses. Marketers grab our attention by appealing to the subliminal, "bottom up" cognitive systems—the brain functions we aren't really aware of. These systems are yanked around by promises of sex, wealth, power, social acceptance, or inclusion. Our bodies are being manipulated: we get a surge of hormonal activity when we respond to images that give us the warm fuzzies (kittens, puppies, babies) or photos designed to enrage us (trophy hunters, violence, environmental destruction). Social platforms are designed to be addictive, and brain-scans show that their use causes heightened activity in the same brain areas as substance abuse and gambling.[8]

As we become caught up by this cognitive crack, we don't have time to explore anything deep, spiritual, or analytical. Hence, the devolution of politics into partisan, child-like name-calling with little appreciation of facts, research, or the complexity of issues. We are drawn to the best entertainers, the best performers, as opposed to the best leaders or problem-solvers. Attention overload blinds us to the manipulation that is creating and sustaining damaging real-world behaviors. When we aren't processing information well, we start to believe bizarre cultural messages, like male virility being reflected by a weed-free lawn.

To generate a following on social media you have to fabricate a brand—an "online self" that lives in the virtual world. Creating this social media "personality" is expensive both energetically and spiritually. It's a type of unpaid work, and generates a soul-cage in which we can't be authentic in case our feelings are inconsistent with the fabrication we're working on. We're constantly self-editing. Some of us are so obsessed with creating just the right picture for Instagram that we're actually not paying attention to the place we're visiting or the people we're with. I have a friend who told me that her obsession with archiving all her "perfect moments" comes from the fear that if she doesn't do so, she'll forget them. And there's truth to that, because if your attention is always divided, you don't have the cognitive capacity to lay down long-term memories.

Friendships online are not the same as friendships offline: there is far too much mediation online, from within and from without. Advocates of social media rave about the ability to connect, but how many of those online "friends" would come pick you up if your car broke down? Connections online might be a way to begin a friendship, but they pale in comparison to spending one-on-one time in the presence of another being.

Is it possible to be authentic on social media? I suppose it is if you color within the lines—if you look the right way, and conform to the right unwritten codes (keep it brief, light, relatable). I think it's really hard for eccentrics and sensitive people. If you deviate from the codes, you risk being trashed, ignored, or excluded. Tribalism evolves easily because nuance and real discussion seldom happen. Also, social media is forever, so if you post something in a lapse of judgment, chances are that in future, someone, somewhere will be able to find it and use it to hurt you.

Research has found that in general, the more time we spend on social media, the unhappier we are. A study by Holly Shakya and Nicholas Christakis indicated that measures of life satisfaction, mental, and physical health all declined with increasing Facebook use.[9] Facebook has also been called "the envy generator," because everyone posts their highlight reels and not the mundane reality of their everyday activities.

According to John Bell and John Zada, "Masters of profits and propaganda are farming our minds, doing cumulative damage that may go to the very core of our humanity. As a result, our attention is becoming locked into a low level of living and functioning."[10]

Chamath Palihapitiya, Facebook's former vice president, would like to see people walk away from social media, because it's "ripping apart the social fabric of how society works."[11] But given the popularity and useful aspects of social media, it's unlikely to be going anywhere soon.

Personally, I find the more I stay away from it, the happier and calmer I feel. At the same time, I think it's possible to use social media without too many destructive side effects, just as it's possible to enjoy a drink without becoming an alcoholic. You can use platforms wisely by limiting your exposure (e.g., set a timer), retaining your skepticism (fact-check), keeping your privacy settings strong, and following only trusted friends and family.

Attention, and, by extension, concentration, is a precious and limited resource. What you spend it on will determine the quality of your experiences, and ultimately your life.

Practice & Reflect

Choose a day when you are not working or required to be checking your phone or email. Make a note of the time.

- Go about your daily routine, whatever that entails, but see how long you can avoid checking your phone or your "socials."
- When you experience the urge to do so, notice what you're feeling in your body, and where you're feeling it.

Journal:
- What thoughts come to mind? What feelings? Fear of missing out? Anxiety? Guilt?

Review the friends you have listed on your social media accounts.

- How many of them are people you'd go out of your way to see in real life? How many of them have you seen or spoken to offline in the last year? The point of this exercise is not to dismiss your social media connections, but rather to contemplate the meaning of "friend" or "relationship" in your own life.

- Now think about how you present on social media. What parts of your personality, or what emotions, do you exclude from your online persona?

We're All Addicted to Something

*Drugs and alcohol are not my problem, reality is my problem,
drugs and alcohol are my solution.*
— Russell Brand

A sweet friend of mine recently lost his mother to lung cancer. We were talking one day about how his grief was playing out, and he described being angry that she had been a heavy smoker despite knowing all the risks and potential outcomes of the behavior. He said something like this: "I can't believe her addiction was more powerful than her brain." In response I asked him to give me his cellphone for the day. You can guess what his reply was.

In short, we're all addicted to something, and the part of the brain that controls judgment is simply not as powerful as the lizard brain that wants what it wants.

In recent years, with advances in brain-imaging technology, and with the internet allowing research to become public knowledge faster than it used to, we've learned a lot about addiction. We've discovered that temperament plays a role, and that children who have difficulty with delayed gratification at the age of five have a higher likelihood of suffering from addiction later in life. We've learned that children can learn to delay gratification with a little help from caring adults. Also, we've discovered physiological differences from person to person that directly affect how prone we are to addictive substances. Finally, we've awakened to the idea that the fundamental cause of addiction is pain—not lack of willpower.

In yoga psychology, we examine the spaces between having a sensation in the body, developing a feeling about it (I like this, I hate this), and taking action. An addiction works something like this: It's dreary and damp outside,

I feel tired and depressed, I don't like the feeling, so I go get myself a piece of chocolate from the leftover Halloween stash. The chocolate gives me a way to feel something I like better. Myriad things achieve the same end—e.g., caffeine, nicotine, potato chips, Facebook, TV, wine—basically anything I find pleasurable. In moderation, none of these things are a problem. If we turn to them habitually and compulsively, however, and if we lose our ability to moderate, all can be damaging to our well-being.

The way we treat addicts, unfortunately, is usually based in judgment and intellectual ideals as opposed to a sophisticated understanding of the complexity of the problem. Historically we've treated addicts as losers who lack self-discipline. We've denied them the benefit of sympathy or curiosity. It's easier not to regard their suffering if we think about them as "less than" or "inferior" to the rest of us. This is not to deny the fact that people with addictions can cause terrible pain and suffering to the people who love them, but rather to say that addiction is complex, and that we're all affected by it.

Our whole culture is addicted to consuming at rates higher than at any other time in human history. According to the International Institute for Sustainable Development, since the 1970s we have been "over-shooting" the natural resources the earth can sustainably regenerate.[12] The amounts of water, soil, minerals, fish, trees, and fuels we consume have been growing at alarming rates and are leading to deforestation, extinctions, loss of biodiversity, pollution, and climate change. "Earth Overshoot Day," the date each year that marks us taking more than nature can regenerate, fell on July 29, 2019, the earliest date since these metrics have been collected.[13] We are "consuming" ourselves to extinction.

Improving attention and concentration are helpful to working with addiction, because they offer a way to interrupt the automatic cycle of stimulus and response that underpins addictive behaviors, whether related to smoking, gambling, eating, or shopping. In yoga and mindfulness practice, we constantly work with our ability to stay present in the face of ever-changing sensations, and to act from a place of deep awareness as opposed to escapism and compulsion. There's nothing inherently wrong with diversion or enjoying the finer things in life—as long as it feels like a choice. The hope is that as we practice more, we develop better awareness of what is driving us, the cheese balls and cocktails become less tempting, and we can consciously decide between self-restraint or indulging in life's little pleasures.

Practice & Reflect

Journal:

- What are you addicted to? When are those addictions most likely to show up? When you're alone? With others?
- Are you addicted to something that you haven't previously thought of as an addiction? Horoscopes? Newsfeeds? Instagram?
- How do you feel about others who have addictions? Choose three descriptive words.
- How do you feel about your own addictions? Choose three descriptive words.

Part Two: Mindfulness

Mindfulness is actually the cultivation of generosity.
The cultivation of compassion. It's being attentive in a way that lets
you recognize intimacy.
— Michael Stone

The second stage on this path to wholeness (which is another way of thinking about equanimity) is developing mindfulness. In Pali (the Buddha's language) the word for mindfulness is *sati*, and in Sanskrit (the language of yoga) it's *smrti*. *Sati* is a verb. It means "to remember" or to "come back." In English we sometimes use the word *mindful* to mean "be careful" or "pay attention." In all cases, the term has an object. We're coming back *to* something. We need the foundation of concentration to be able to pay attention to the task at hand—coming back to our awareness of our bodies, our minds, our feelings, and whatever else is going on around us. We're developing the ability to differentiate between our thoughts about things, and the things in themselves.

The point of mindfulness is not to live constantly in the present moment—that's impossible. Rather, mindfulness is a skill that we can use to become aware of the places we're stuck, or scared, or unwilling to explore.

We come face to face with our inner angels and demons, over and over. And doing so, we develop acceptance, kindness, and a better sense of humor.

Mindfulness meditation is the principal practice of Buddhism and is practiced in yoga within the "limb" of dhyana. Although the two traditions use different languages, and sometimes different anchor-points, from the outside the "sitting" looks identical. In both traditions it operates as a tool that we can use to work with a much larger set of teachings called the dharma, or yoga.

Mindfulness asks us to develop steadiness in our attention, and then use that ability to look at the ways we're living, the ways we're loving, and the state of the world that we're living in. Benefits of mindfulness include more gratitude, more authenticity, and the ability to "be" with what is difficult. Although we use meditation practice as a place to build our mindfulness muscle, once we get the hang of it, we can practice anywhere at any time.

Practice & Reflect

Journal:

- What are your feelings about mindfulness? Be honest, e.g., "Sounds great, but I don't have time."

- What images come to mind when you read or hear or visualize the word mindfulness?

- If you've tried meditating in the past and quit, ask yourself, "What stopped me?" Write down every reason you can think of.

The Tidal Pull Toward Awakening

*There's a path from me to You
I'm constantly looking for
So I try to keep clear and still
As water does with the moon.*
— Rumi

The human brain is a master of anticipation and a sense-making machine. The yogis imagined the mind divided into two parts: one part to look after the pragmatic "animal," or survival functions, and a second "spiritual" part that longs to return home to something whole, expansive, and unaffected by the cycle of life and death. Every religion echoes this longing, although each has a different way of imagining the perfect wholeness that is the reward for an ethical and unselfish life.

Even those who have no religious beliefs or affiliations have a deeply instinctive drive toward meaning and belonging. We tell our stories based on the archetype of the hero's journey. We can't envision a life without some sort of narrative movement, without some growth and change over the passage of time. In virtually every tale the hero encounters a predicament, or meets with an imperative that requires a quest. Obstacles arise, suffering ensues, but in the end there is learning, expansion, and satisfaction. Usually, also, there is homecoming, and a new appreciation for having a home.

The Buddha's story is such a quest. The young Siddhartha Gautama was over-protected and sheltered by his parents because of a prophecy. When he escaped as a young man, he was shocked to encounter old age, sickness, and death—and took off on a mission to come to terms with this disturbing (to him) situation. His journey took years and included many hardships, but after nearly dying from austere yoga practices, he decided to sit down under a Bhodi tree and stay, unmoving, until he either died or came to terms with his suffering. And when he stopped trying, when he stopped moving and fully surrendered, he had an epiphany. His ideas about the path out of suffering became clear to him, and he made his way home.

The Buddhist word for the drive toward wholeness and meaning is bodhicitta. Bodhi means "to wake up, to be open, to be in the light"; and citta means "mind/heart" or "consciousness." Bodhicitta is the source of the inner voice that whispers "there's more," or "there's something you need to learn." But this particular hero's journey asks that rather than getting busier, running off on adventures, or traveling the world, you sit down in the middle of your life, right where you already are. This journey goes inward, through the mountains and oceans of your psyche to your deeply embedded thought patterns, habits, and drives.

We all have this desire, and this capacity to become whole. Often it functions at cross-purposes with our drive toward safety, continuity, and stability. Our motivation to connect with our "spirit" can conflict with what's good for the economy, or cultural norms like striving after wealth, status, or escapism. But bodhicitta is a powerful urge, which gets louder in times of stress or pain. We can listen or not. But in the Yoga and Buddhist traditions, it requires that we stop running, stop talking, and aim toward what is clear and still.

Practice & Reflect

Journal:

- Do you ever feel pulled toward a different life? What does that life look like?
- In what specific ways would your life differ from the one you're living now?
- How do you imagine those differences would feel?

Simple But Not Easy

It is the simple things in life that are the most extraordinary.
— Paul Coelho

Imagine you've committed to taking up mindfulness. You sit down in a comfortable chair, soften your gaze, and tune in to the feeling and movement of your breath. And your mental dialogue goes something like this:

> Breathing in, breathing out. Inhale, exhale …did I remember to take the chicken out of the freezer? Oops. Inhale, exhale. I'm pretty sure I did, but did I accidentally leave it on the counter? Maybe I should go check …It should be okay for ten minutes. But what if the cat gets into it? I'm sure I put it in the fridge. Okay. Inhale, exhale. Now I'm inhaling, now I'm exhaling. Maybe I should make lemon chicken instead of barbecue. Wow, I really suck at this …oh wait, I'm not supposed to be critical…

Welcome to mindfulness practice: an incredibly simple technique that's incredibly difficult to master. Truth be told, it might be described as a practice of repetitive failure with moments of delightful clarity and calm. Learning to be gentle and non-judgmental with yourself is just as important as learning to stay with the breath.

In recent years mindfulness is being celebrated as the cure for all that ails you. Secular mindfulness has become extremely popular with the medical and neuroscience community because of its benefits for reducing stress and improving focus, and its helpfulness to other psychotherapies. With the advent of advanced brain scanning, such as Functional Magnetic Resonance

Imaging, scientists have been able to study and compare the brains of meditators and non-meditators, and have been able to demonstrate physical differences in the brain structures and abilities of advanced meditators.

With this burgeoning interest, and the widespread availability of online trainings in meditation, anyone with a Wi-Fi connection can learn to sit. At the same time, what can be lost are the contextual teachings, traditions, and teacher–student relationships that historically accompanied these trainings. In other words, meditation was meant to be part of a much bigger picture that helped you to know what to do with your mind, once you began to know it better. Every meditation-based tradition has a slightly different take on how mindfulness should be practiced. The Vipassana tradition describes practice as having two wings: the first is a calm, attentive solidity (comparable to yoga's dharana) called shamata; and the second is the ability to investigate, observe, and develop an inward-focused appreciation of how your consciousness works, known as vipassana (vi = in, passa= eye), or "insight."

The Zen tradition, in contrast, eschews conceptual ideas about process and describes meditation practice as "just sitting," or shikentaza. Shunryu Suzuki said that sitting and enlightenment are essentially the same thing: You don't become enlightened by sitting; rather, you are enlightened because you sit. In both Vipassana and Zen, the reward of practice is the recognition of the interconnectedness of all things, including you.

There are countless meditation techniques available, and although I will introduce you to a few of them in this book, my intent is not to offer a "how to." When I work with students, we choose a technique and work with it for a sustained period. If they run into issues, we try something different, or modify what they're doing. The practice of mindfulness is rich, sometimes frustrating, sometimes magical, and ever-changing: it requires patience, commitment, and support.

Practice & Reflect

Practice:
- Set timer for five minutes.
- Sit quietly in a comfortable chair.
- Soften your gaze, or close your eyes.
- Choose one place in your body where you can feel breath moving easily. Often, the openings of the nostrils work well, or the lower ribs, or the abdomen.
- Whatever area you choose, focus your attention there, and see if you can stay with the sensation of breath as you inhale, and then as you exhale.
- Focus on this one place, but notice how each phase of the breath brings subtle shifts in what you notice. You might observe, perhaps, that in the nostrils, the inhalation follows a slightly different route than the exhalation.
- After the timer goes off, take a moment to connect with your body and notice how you are feeling physically, emotionally, and energetically.

A Time and A Place — Some Cautionary Notes

Smile, breathe and go slowly.
— Thich Nhat Hahn

Once during a weekend retreat, I was sitting in meditation and began to experience a strange, though not unpleasant, tingling in my body, which grew larger and more all-encompassing until it felt electrifying. Having read about "Kundalini" experiences, I decided that must be what it was, and felt rather pleased with myself—like I'd accomplished something. But it occurred to me, too, that if I hadn't already heard of this, I might have been terrified. Later, when I talked to my teacher about it, he said, "Yeah, that happens. You should ignore it."

"What do you mean?" I asked.

He said, "It's a distraction; it's not the main event. And if you enjoyed it you can make yourself suffer for years trying to make it happen again."

And it felt like he knew me all too well, because I did enjoy the experience and would have been happy if it happened daily. And chasing after that would have been just as harmful as all the other habits I'd been trying to let go of.

Although I am a huge proponent of mindfulness, I think it's important to acknowledge that it's not for everybody, and that for some people, at certain times, it can be harmful. For people struggling with severe depression, for example, a sitting practice may be one more place to ruminate, and that's not something that a teacher or class leader can observe. And for people coping with trauma, some instructions, like leaning in to a difficult emotion, could be more harmful than helpful. For those who already have trouble staying grounded in reality, long periods of meditation can trigger hallucinations or feelings of disembodiment. In some monastic traditions, new monks spend years learning and reading before they're even allowed to start practicing meditation. Their teachers and mentors make sure they know the novices thoroughly before allowing them to start working with their minds.

Dr. Willoughby Britton, a neuroscience researcher and mindfulness practitioner, has become an expert in identifying and treating the harmful side-effects of meditation. Her research has shown that side-effects have been documented around the world, and many are described in ancient texts. They range from sensory hypersensitivity, to disorientation and confusion, to emotional disturbances, to losing a sense of relationship to time. These symptoms can happen within a few days, or even after many years of practice. Although they are relatively rare, it's important that support and help are available.[1]

The obvious question is "How do I know if practicing mindfulness will be good for me?" We all seem to have a huge resistance to sitting still, even if we turn out to be perfectly suited to it—so liking or disliking it isn't the best measure. The advice I give my students is to start slow, with short practice periods, and pay attention to what's happening both mentally and emotionally. If strong or unusual feelings occur, it might be better to try a different practice (like physical yoga), change the environment, or switch to another technique. Trial and error seems to be the best way to go, and talking to a teacher about what comes up for you is really helpful.

Also, mindfulness may be for you, but not now. Sometimes it's the other problems and conditions in our lives that are the issue. People who are suffering from a loss might in theory benefit from practicing mindfulness, but not while they're enduring the early stages of grief. Or there's the risk that meditation techniques can be misused to avoid feeling unpleasant emotions, which is known as "spiritual bypassing," and can lead to longer-term issues with coping. Or you may have more pragmatic problems, like having a couple of little ones at home. In that case your mindfulness practice might be five minutes in bed before you fall asleep at night. Remember this path toward equanimity has seven parts, and mindfulness might not happen until some of the other pieces come together. Meditation is a powerful tool, but like any other tool, it needs to be used with care and respect.

Practice & Reflect

If you struggle with sitting still, here is a different practice to try:

- Pick an activity that you already do every day, like taking a shower.
- Next time you take a shower, make a commitment to be fully attentive to everything you're doing and feeling.
- Instead of planning the rest of your day, for example, focus on the sensation of the water against your skin, the scent of your shampoo, the sequence of soaping and rinsing, and so on.
- When your mind wanders, bring it back to what you're doing. Try to be fully present.

Motivation to Meditate
(When You Don't Feel Like It)

Meditation is not a means to an end.
It is both the means and the end.
— Krishnamurti

Any meditator or person who has engaged in an ongoing spiritual or personal growth practice will at times feel it seems pointless, or boring, or disappointing. A few years ago I was going through one of these periods, when the group I practice with invited the Zen teacher, poet, and translator Peter Levitt to instruct us for a weekend. We each had the opportunity to sit down with him one-on-one to ask questions about our meditation practice and any obstacles we were wrestling with. One thing I remember with particular fondness is that these meetings took place in a broom closet; it was the only place we had that was private. When I call it to mind I envision Peter sitting on his meditation cushion surrounded by folding chairs, mops and paper towels—like a cave-dwelling guru with a cleaning fetish.

Most of us shared similar issues. We know that meditation practice helps us, but we struggle to fit it in. Our lives are crazy busy, and taking time out to just sit and breathe feels self-indulgent and not as important as dealing with the demands of work, family, or email. When we do have a moment to breathe, we often feel a resistance—irrational and un-nameable—to sitting on the cushion. We know that meditation does wonders for our concentration, our outlook, and our sense of compassion. We know it's good for us, and still we resist. The call of the snooze button is louder than our call to awakening.

Peter was generous with his time and his answers. First, he was clear that we just have to do it anyway, whether we like it or hate it. We have to trust that what feels like the desert is actually full of life, and stop expecting our lives to be different from what they are. Second, he pointed out that the part of us that clings to habit doesn't like meditation. The part caught up in egotism and separation and "the story of me" really doesn't like it much when we get real. He said, "If we're not careful, we might have to change."

After I explained my feeling of losing heart, he asked me to reflect on who benefits when I'm practicing. I thought about it and replied that I do, and my friends and family, and my students, and my community. Then he asked, "Who benefits if you pack it in and give up?" And the list included polluters, warmongers, racists, bullies, and every other force in the world that promotes hatred, greed, and delusion.

"So do you think you need to keep going?" he said.

"Hmm. Good point," I said.

After coming out of our closet meeting, I reconsidered the importance of getting down on the cushion and tackling the delusions in my own heart and mind—especially the parts that feel pulled back to shopping, or Facebook, or creating barriers between "us and them," or wanting to be powerful, or worry-free, or irresponsible. The gravitational pull of culture is hard to see and harder to resist. We all crave security, safety, comfort, control, influence, and recognition. We're all caught up in a process of "self-improvement" that has the potential to lead us farther away from what is beautiful and boundless.

The weekend was a reminder to be okay with just being. A reminder to recognize that we live in and have to function in a world of duality (us vs. them, good vs. bad, economy vs. environment), while at the same time realizing that none of these divisions exist in the way we think they do. Even when "I" don't feel like practicing, there is something much bigger and much more beautiful that needs tending. I was making it about me, when it really has nothing to do with me at all. Or rather, I've been thinking about myself in a small and narrow way, instead of the me that contains and is held by everything.

Practice & Reflect

Journal:

- Think about a goal or a new habit that you've been struggling to incorporate into your routine. Write it down.
- List the ways in which achieving this goal would benefit you.
- See if you can think of at least one other person or organization who might benefit.
- How would they benefit? Be as specific as you can.

The Art of Intimate Surveillance

You do not know what wars are going on down there
Where the spirit meets the bone.
— Lucinda Williams

Let me start with a confession. I did not come up with the term *intimate surveillance*. I heard it on CBC Radio used in the context of relationship strife. Apparently stealing your partner's cellphone password and monitoring their social media is a thing these days. But when I heard the term, it jumped out for a different reason.

A great deal of neuroscientific research focuses on capacities that can improve with mindfulness training. "Interoception" describes the ability to bring sustained awareness to whatever feelings and sensations are going on in our internal organs or "viscera." We could describe this tuning in to "gut feeling" as intimate surveillance, and it is a capability that can be improved with training.

Recognizing what you feel can be surprisingly difficult. Some people are well attuned to their inner states, but for many of us it's like trying to listen to a distant radio signal—there's a lot of static and interference. Usually when a feeling comes into awareness, the mind immediately gets involved, and the parts of our psychology that make stories and pass judgments set to work building a narrative to go with it. When we're offered a new position at work, we might not be able to decide whether our anxiety is based in excitement about the challenge or whether it's a signal that the added responsibility might become a nightmare.

When we're confused about what we feel, we rationalize. We agonize. We look externally for reassurance or affirmation. Our wounds and our life experiences also alter and influence what we *can* feel. Perhaps you were raised in a family where boys weren't allowed to cry, or girls weren't allowed to ask for what they want. Perhaps you were an extrovert in a family of introverts, or a sensitive boy in a family of macho men. Most of us have feelings that we disallow and disavow.

To complicate matters further, suffering from trauma and neglect at some point in our histories can physically alter the way we experience emotions. More and more research demonstrates that powerful emotional events can be literally written into our bodies. When emotions feel too overwhelming to process, the body can bury them or convert them to stress syndromes that cause more suffering. An alarming number of veterans, police officers, and paramedics commit suicide or are unable to work because of what they've witnessed or had to deal with in their line of duty. A series of calamities can literally break the heart, causing a frightening, although temporary, syndrome called Takotsubo Cardiomyopathy.

Yoga teaches us to be intimate with whatever is arising in the present moment. First, we learn to identify sensations in the body, and then gradually we learn to stay still. As our ability to pay attention and concentrate grows, we can cultivate the ability to stay with feelings without reaching for our cellphones or the ice cream in the freezer. If the feelings that come up are powerful or overwhelming, the support of a teacher and a referral to a good therapist can be important steps on the path to emotional recovery.

Once we develop the ability to stay, we can start incorporating the tools provided in the yoga sutras that move us toward friendliness, compassion, generosity, and equanimity. To be who we truly are, we have to feel what we truly feel. We have to be able to distinguish what we really want from the confusion of what we're told we should want. We need to learn the practice of intimate surveillance so that we can be true to the call of our spontaneous, deep, and authentic self, however eccentric that might be.

This is simple, but not easy. We start with the most elemental exercises: Place your body in this position. What do you feel? It takes patience and time. It definitely takes commitment. But if you are willing to take the plunge, you'll find more to explore in your inner world than you ever thought or imagined.

Practice & Reflect

Journal:

- Write down one "feeling state" that you are struggling with, or have struggled with in the past, such as jealousy, or feeling left out, or feeling misunderstood.

- Remember the feeling (as opposed to a particular incident), and then write down three areas of your body affected by that feeling. For example, when I feel envious, my neck feels hunched, my heart feels heavy, my eye muscles tighten.

- Now choose a happy or uplifting feeling and repeat the exercise.

Form Versus Substance

*The only Zen you find on the tops of mountains is the
Zen you bring up there.*
— Robert M. Pirsig

When we decide to meditate for the first time, we often visualize the Buddha or some gorgeous yoga model perched in full Lotus Pose. After sitting for a few minutes in the closest approximation our bodies can achieve, we discover that our hips and spines are not pleased. Usually we end up in agony by about minute four.

Because I trained with a Buddhist (Vipassana/Zen) teacher, I teach my students the traditional upright sitting posture: sitting on a cushion or bench, with the pelvis rotated slightly forward/downward so that the lumbar spine naturally curves and the knees drop lower than the hips. For students with tight hips or arthritic knees, I recommend sitting on a chair with the feet firmly on the ground (or supported) with the spine upright (i.e., not leaning on the back of the chair). Some yoga schools and systems of meditation do not care about form in the slightest, but I have tried to meditate without form, and my personal experience is that it is a worthwhile pursuit.

Most people experience some discomfort at first with this upright position. Often we have to fight the tendency to slouch, and the muscles of the spine and shoulders can get angry and painful. As a guideline, if the pain starts within the first five minutes, and becomes all you can think about, it's best to change position. But if the pain is slow to arise, and not terrible, it can be an interesting study to just observe and watch it, treating it as a sensation, staying with it and attending to how it changes and moves, while continually coming back to breathing. Like any yoga posture, the more often you do it, and the more consistently, the easier it will be. But you need to achieve a balance between effort and self-care; and nobody is a better judge of that balance than you.

Here are a few of the most common questions I hear and answer:

Q: *Why can't I just lie down?*

A: Technically you can lie down, but the reality is that 99.9 percent of adults will fall asleep within microseconds of assuming a comfortable reclined posture. (I didn't do an empirical study; this is based on observation and personal experience.) If you don't fall asleep immediately, you are still more likely to be distracted by daydreaming and drifting about in your thoughts. Mindfulness meditation is different from relaxation. The whole idea is to stay awake and pay attention. Falling asleep is a sure-fire way to check out before things get interesting. On the other hand, if you really need to lie down, you can try lying with your elbows bent so that your forearms, wrists, and hands point straight up toward the ceiling. If you fall asleep, they will flop down and wake you up.

Q: *What about leaning on the wall or the back of the chair?*

A: This can be a useful technique if you absolutely cannot tolerate upright sitting, but again, it may relax you too much. Sometimes it's helpful to start in the unsupported, upright posture, and then, when you lose your tolerance for it, you can lean back. In this practice, body and mind are viewed as one and the same, and a loose, floppy posture can encourage the mind to wander. In any case, you are the judge and jury. You must decide whether you're just feeling lazy or whether you really need to adjust in order to alleviate pain in your spine.

Q: *My legs fall asleep—what should I do?*

A: Remember that although it is uncomfortable when this happens, it is not usually fatal, and so far we haven't had to do any amputations. Generally if your leg falls asleep, you should quietly and calmly change position. The most important thing is to take your time getting up, so that you don't fall on your face. Make sure you are not wearing restrictive clothing, and give it time. Most of the time it is just a flexibility issue and improves the more often you sit. Doing some yoga to loosen up before sitting can be helpful too. Alternatively, you could try a taller cushion, or switch to a kneeling bench or chair.

Q: *What should I do if I feel faint or nauseated?*

A: I've had it happen, and witnessed it happen to others, particularly on retreats where we do early morning sits before breakfast. Don't stand up or run for the bathroom, because this can cause a blackout. The best practice is to ease yourself off your cushion or chair and just lie down until the feeling passes.

Bodily discomfort is a normal part of learning to meditate, and each individual situation is different. Some students push through, and others need to respect the discomfort and modify their position.

The formal sitting posture is a bit of an art form. Creating it demands discipline, concentration, and time. Peter Levitt compares form to preparing a canvas before you paint on it. The time and care that goes into the form will affect what becomes possible in the overall practice. Once you've developed really good form, the physical part of sitting becomes effortless. As with any art form (music, painting, writing), it is necessary in meditation to fully understand and appreciate the technical skills and rules before deciding to deviate from them. Only out of commitment and mastery can fluidity and creativity be achieved.

In meditation practice, the body and mind are not separate. Together they are the form and the substance, both the arena where the work is done and the work itself. Whether you sit in full Lotus, or on a chair, or lie on the floor, what's important is that all of your being stays present. And that takes commitment, lots of practice, and self-compassion.

Practice & Reflect

Meditation:

- Set timer for ten minutes. Transition into your preferred meditation position.

- Starting at your feet, notice every sensation that you can. Are your feet taking equal amounts of weight? Which parts of your feet feel more connected to the floor? Are they warm or cool? What textures do you feel on or around them?

- Continue on with this mental inventory of sensations, working your way up the body, until the timer goes off.

Tapas: The Space Where Change Can Happen

The supreme purpose of Tapas is to accept life's challenges while being loving and compassionate to all, especially ourselves.
— Nischala Joy Devi

In the second portion (pada) of the yoga sutras, Patanjali describes a practice called kriya yoga, or "the yoga of action." The word *kriya* is related to *karma*, and the English word *create*. Kriya yoga consists of three parts: *tapas* (effort), *svadyaya* (study), and *ishvara pranidana* (surrender).

The word *tapas* is translated as "discipline, fire, or austerity" (unless you're Spanish, in which case it's a form of cuisine). Any time you want to make a change, learn something new, or grow, tapas is needed. There is a sense of patience and stillness to tapas, however; it's not so much about enthusiasm as it is about staying power. Meditation practice is one of the most useful and powerful arenas in which to work on this ability.

My teacher once said that the word *tapas* originates from the days of temple fires. The homeowner in ancient India would pay the local priests (Brahmins) to make sure that the sacrificial fire was attended to properly, so that it wouldn't go out or burn the house down. The fire needed careful monitoring, sustained for the lifetime of the homeowner. The same could be said of heating by wood-stove. But the word *tapas* is also translated sometimes as "pain."

Tapas could be described as the skill of being able to monitor feelings and emotions, without automatically falling back on our habits of desire, aversion, storytelling, or delusional thinking. In this instance, *tapas* means the ability to interrupt the flow of automatic thoughts and habit loops. It means to sit unmoving in the midst of our compulsions and to trust in the emergence of a solution, or as my teacher used to say, "Let the door open from the other side."

Yoga teacher Richard Freeman talks about tapas as a type of alertness that happens when we enter a physical or psychological space that is sacred. He also describes tapas as the ability to be okay with paradox, to be able to stand between two seeming opposites and see that both can be true. Only in that moment of suspension can new possibilities arise.[2]

Back in high school, we used to have debates as part of our curriculum. We would argue about one side of an issue and then we would switch sides and make the opposite case. Not only was this a great practice for developing empathy, but also it made us recognize that most things are never simple or clear, and that our knowledge is always limited by the lens of our personal circumstances and history. It was a good foundation for tapas and for playing well with others.

Developing tapas means exercising and building our tolerance for ambiguity. It's about being able to ask a question without expecting an answer, and being able to not-know without being overcome by anxiety.

Tapas allows us to explore mind-body states, while at the same time unhooking from the reflexive cycles that we can get stuck in. Tapas requires dedicating time to awareness, contemplation, or exploration, and then feeling the personality's resistance and irritation (the proverbial heat) without running away or falling into our default escape hatches (Netflix, anyone?). In our frenetic society, we most often need tapas when we are asked to sit still; otherwise focus is impossible. If we can maintain concentration, we start to notice the sources of our suffering, and can explore new and different ways of navigating our lives and relationships.

Practice & Reflect

Meditation:

- For seven days in a row, pick a specific time of day, and sit down on your cushion or chair.
- Set timer for fifteen minutes.

- Sit up straight, soften your gaze (or close your eyes) and bring your attention to the movement of your breath. You can choose a particular focal point (e.g., the belly) or observe the whole series of movements that accompany the inhale and the exhale.
- Notice what thoughts and feelings arise, but then come back to just breathing and feeling sensations.
- When you become aware of being distracted, come back your breathing without beating yourself up. Just keep starting over.

Journal:

- When the timer goes off, take five minutes to write down any strong or repetitive thoughts or feelings that emerged. Don't go into detail, just name the predominant ones.
- Circle those that are pleasurable, and underline those that are unpleasant or aversive.
- If you have neutral thoughts or feelings, just leave them uncategorized.
- After doing this for a week, go back over your list and see if you notice any patterns. Write down any insights or *aha*'s.

Mindful Insomnia

What do sheep count when they can't sleep?
— Anon

The second line of the yoga sutra says "Yoga citta vritti nirodha," which loosely translated means, "Yoga stills the churning of consciousness." There's no better time to experience the churning of consciousness than at three in the morning when you're lying in bed wide awake, feeling anxious, watching the minutes tick by.

As an experienced insomniac, I've experimented with myriad techniques for trying to get to sleep (or back to sleep). Of course, some of the common tips such as keeping a regular routine and not watching screens after dark, while helpful, are not possible for most people (particularly if you are one of the many whose employment spills over into the evening hours). Also, there are conflicting opinions in the literature about the best techniques to use—whether you should just lie awake in bed, or whether 'tis nobler to get up and do some ironing. Sometimes insomnia is a result of hormonal changes (e.g., menopause) or simply a lack of exercise.

New research has discovered that the brain flushes itself out while we sleep, and that this cleaning process may be important in the prevention of illnesses like Alzheimer's. Sleep also allows our brains to integrate and file away what we've experienced during the day, and our dreams can give us useful emotional insights from parts of the brain we don't ordinarily pay attention to. The more we learn about the functions of sleep, the more we realize that it's critical for good health and immunity.

We live in anxiety-inducing times, in a culture that encourages us to never sit, never stop, and always be available. Watching the news, we witness wars and calamities all around us, as well as environmental devastation, social upheaval, and dire economic forecasts. We'd like to isolate ourselves from the pain of others, but sometimes the more we try to do that, the more we cut ourselves off from our own interiority. We're porous creatures, and whatever we're trying to repress finds other avenues to seep through. Often, annoyingly, all the difficult thoughts and feelings that accumulate during the course of our day seem to show up for deeper "processing" in the middle of the night.

Mindfulness encourages us to focus on just feeling what we're feeling. Not trying to make it go away. Not trying to fix it, but also learning not to feed into it, not to make it worse. When we can make space for those anxious, scary feelings, we can recognize that they come and go. They are transient. And when we stop running away and really spend some time with them, they lose a lot of their control over us. Anxious feelings are just as normal as all the other types of feelings; the trick is in learning what to do when we feel them. We can learn to go to the places that scare us and come safely home again.

I know of a few ways to work with anxious feelings in the night. One of my favorites is just to stop, take a breath, and put a "label" on it. I'll sometimes say, "Hi, anxiety, it's not a good time, but I hear you knocking." Instead of exploring the thoughts and stories that are provoking it, I'll go into my body and see if I can pinpoint exactly where I'm feeling the anxiety. There's often a tightening in my jaw, and a feeling of heaviness between my eyebrows. Then I'll work on those physical manifestations—by sticking out my tongue. My husband usually manages to sleep through all of this, and in case you're wondering, I don't talk to anxiety out loud.

Another mantra I use is this: "There's nothing I can do about ____ at three in the morning." It doesn't always work, but it's worth a try. Also, sometimes it's helpful to zoom out from a time perspective, and ask, "How much will this matter to me five years from now?"

Insomnia causes us suffering, but it can also be an important warning sign—an indicator that we have psychological work to do, or that there are aspects of our life we need to re-examine. Sometimes it's just a signal from the body that we're doing too much, and taking in more stimuli than it's possible for our body-minds to digest. Rather than taking sedatives, which might be a short-term solution but become a long-term problem, we can view lying awake at night as an opportunity to practice. Learning to stay with the breath and bodily sensations, and not get hooked by the content of our thoughts, can be a good use of our insomniac time. Of course, seeking professional help and long-term solutions like psychotherapy may be necessary, but those aren't things you can do at three in the morning. Reframing insomnia as a signal that something inside you is trying to awaken is a useful way to take back your sense of agency and find the tools you need to return to restful sleep.

Practice & Reflect

The following two practices from yoga are helpful in down-regulating the nervous system. They use the body to tell the vagus nerve to switch into "rest and digest" mode.

Extended exhale at the best beach you can imagine:

- Start by visualizing a beautiful and calm beach setting. If you're a "cold" person, imagine lying on warm sand. If you're a "hot" person, imagine lying in cool water.
- Soften your body and sink a little bit deeper into your supportive surface.
- Inhale gently, purse your lips to create a mild resistance, and then exhale in three parts— softly blowing out all the air that you can.
- As your lungs empty, step by step, imagine feeling heavier and wider. The earth or water below you rises to cradle and hold your weight.
- Pause at the end of the exhale, and then inhale normally. (If you feel short of breath or anxious, back off the effort.)
- Repeat five to twelve times.

Legs Up the Wall:

- Caution: This pose is not recommended for people with uncontrolled high blood pressure.

- Find a wall with some clear space on it.
- Sit down so that your legs are parallel to the wall. You should be as close to the wall as possible, but if you have tight hamstrings leave a gap of six to twelve inches.
- As you lie down, pivot your hips so that your legs are up and supported by the wall

- If your hamstrings are tight, you may need to move a few inches away from the wall. The position should feel comfortable and relaxed.
- For more comfort, you can also do this pose with your calves resting on the seat of a chair (rather than the wall).
- Stay for five minutes.

The Princess and the Bodhi Seed

There once lived a beautiful, shining princess who had skin like ebony and a deep, musical laugh. She made her home in the forest, in a tree house that spired up seven stories, and her kingdom was lush and as green as emeralds. Her parents had retired to a district near the ocean, and had left her in charge of diplomacy, the economy, and the welfare of her citizens.

She did what was expected of her, and inspired the respect and loyalty of her subjects. Although she felt the weight of her responsibilities, she loved her kingdom and often took her morning tea on the balcony gazing out over the verdant hills, enjoying the profusion of sounds made by the animals in the jungle below.

One morning her chief security guard informed her of a visitor who had been turned away three days in a row, but who insisted that he must have an audience. The guard had been torn between granting the man's request and putting him in jail, and decided to leave the decision up to the princess. The princess was curious and agreed to meet the man out in the courtyard.

He was flanked by guards and could barely walk. She guessed that his age must be at least a hundred, and his body was stooped, bony, and tremulous. But when he gazed at her his eyes were bright, and a smile burst across his face like a sunrise. She ordered her attendants to bring him a chair and some coffee. And then she sat down across from him.

"What do you want of me?" she asked. "I understand you've been waiting three days."

"My time, my child, is growing short. I was afraid that I'd die before my request was granted. But this matter is of grave importance, and the survival of the kingdom depends on it."

One of the guards made an amused face, to which the princess responded with a glare. She turned back to the old man. "Tell me then," she said.

The old man fumbled in a pocket of his cloak and drew from it a small envelope, with a pea-sized seed inside of it. "This," he gestured shakily, "is the ancient seed of the bodhi tree. It is the ancestor of every being now living, and also, the seed of every death yet to come. I have tended it carefully since it came into my family, and now it is time for it to pass to a worthy guardian. It is a living and sensing thing, which needs to stay close to its keeper."

The princess held out her hand to accept it. She could see that her courtiers were skeptical, but at the same time she felt that the man was not lying. The seed was oddly heavy, and she felt a pulsating energy in her palm as she wrapped her fingers around it. The old man looked relieved to be rid of it. He gestured for her to lean in.

"You must keep it with you, especially at night, and care for it as though your life depended on it, because the life of every sentient being—every child, every insect, every monkey, every plant—relies on the existence of this seed. Without the seed of death, there can be no new life. The wheel of birth and death must turn, and everything that is conceived contains the seed of its dissolution within. When you're old like me, you will understand the gift in this."

"Where would you have me keep it?" she asked, carefully returning the seed to the envelope.

The old man hesitated. "Under your mattress," he said. "It should feel safe and cared for there."

The princess agreed and took her leave, asking her manservant to transport the man home. She returned to her room and tucked the envelope under her mattress, musing that she was apt to forget about it there, but that it wouldn't come to any harm as long as she remembered to tell the maid who laundered the sheets.

The rest of her day proceeded as normal, but once she crawled into bed that evening, she could not find a comfortable position. She tossed and turned and lay awake the entire night. She tried again the following night, but her insomnia was unceasing.

After three nights she called in the royal physician, who decided her mattress needed replacing and ordered a new one stuffed with the finest down. She was certain she would not feel the seed after she'd carefully tucked it into place. But still, no sleep.

Then they tried a second mattress on top of the first, but still the princess couldn't get any rest. She consulted the court philosopher, who suggested another mattress, stuffed with the finest and wisest papers and essays ever written. But no success. She called in the alchemist, who insisted on adding another mattress filled with gold to provide a secure foundation for all the other layers. Still, no improvement. In desperation, she checked with the court jester, who provided a mattress filled with jokes, stories, and pretty pictures. "Diversion is the cure for many ailments," he said, nodding wisely. But still the princess couldn't sleep.

Eventually, she confided her exasperation to the morning maid. "I think this seed might be the death of me."

"Why don't you track down the old man who gave it to you? Perhaps he'll know what to do."

The princess could see the wisdom in this and dispatched the palace guards to go find him. They returned hours later, not with the old man, but with an equally aged and haggard woman whom they had to carry in a sedan chair. They lowered her down in front of the princess.

The old woman coughed. "My husband passed away the day after he came to you. He had been unwell for a very long time."

"Oh dear," said the princess, "I'm so sorry for your loss. But I wonder if you can help me. When your late husband came to me, he brought me a seed. He insisted that I keep it close at night and told me to place it under my mattress. But I find it so irritating, feeling it there, that I haven't been able to sleep ever since."

The rheumy old woman gazed up at the princess and then fumbled with the bodice of her worn and faded dress. She dug a locket out from between her breasts and asked for help to undo the clasp from behind her neck. With her knobby fingers she handed the locket to the princess and nodded at her to open it. Inside was a small picture of the elderly man, back when he was virile and handsome.

"Please give me back the picture," said the old woman, "but keep the locket. If you want to make peace with the bodhi seed, the place to keep it is right next to your heart. My beloved husband was a kind and responsible man, but he never paid enough attention to details. I told him to take the seed to you—but I didn't think to give him the locket."

The princess placed the seed inside the locket, and placed the locket next to her heart, and from that night onward, she slept like a cat in the sun.

Part Three: Investigation

Look at your life. Closely. Notice your mind states. Notice your heart states. And also, if you want to be happy, make sure you're really taking care of things. Like goodness, and sweetness, and love and compassion.[1]
— Craig Hase and Devon Hase

The first two stages of this path are about developing a tool, a mirror of sorts, that we can use to look deeply into our experience. Mindfulness, as we grow more skilled, helps us to develop a level of calm and acceptance of the thoughts and emotions that constantly swirl around in our inner world. Mindfulness doesn't make them go away, but rather loosens up their hold on us so that we can develop humor, curiosity, and abundant gentleness toward ourselves and others. We can recognize that the thoughts and the thinker are not the same thing, and that we are more than what we imagine ourselves to be. But mindfulness is not the end game. There's a Buddhist joke that if you make mindfulness the final goal, you can go from being an idiot to being a calmer idiot. Clearly, there's more to be done.

Once we develop basic steadiness, patience, and a sense of perspective, we can turn our attention to our ways of being in the world. We begin to investigate and develop insight, not only about our selves but also about the nature of reality. As time passes we see that everything is in constant flux, and that our mental models of our selves, our relationships, and the rhythms of life may not be as real or as solid as we believed they were. Although they feel real, when we examine them closely, our perceptions are often not true.

As we venture into unfamiliar territory, we can return to concentration and mindfulness the way a toddler returns to his parent for reassurance. And we can explore the well-worn paths of any or all of the world's great wisdom traditions, knowing that eventually, they all arrive at the same destination.

Practice & Reflect

Journal:

- Imagine you are about to meet a famous guru or saint whom you've admired for a long time.
- You are allowed to ask them three questions.
- What are your three questions?

Impermanence and the Fear of Life

Everything I've ever let go of has claw marks in it.
— David Foster Wallace

The other day, in the midst of roasting beets, I noticed for the first time that our stove has a button on it that says "Stop Time." I wondered to myself: a) How have I never noticed this before? And b) What would it mean to be able to stop time?

Impermanence is something life will teach you if you get to stay around long enough. Often we are pleased and stimulated by changes, like new jobs, new relationships, or even learning a new skill. But impermanence means that we're not always gaining—we're also losing jobs, losing people we love, being forced to deal with situations that we can't control and don't want to be in.

People's encounters with impermanence vary widely. For many of us, bereavement and loss are what give us the motivation to seek out meaning and spiritual practices. Personally, I started this journey at a young age. Three of my four grandparents died before I was born. My Uncle Vin, whom I adored, died when I was fourteen, and during my five years in high school, at least six people I knew were killed, mainly in car and motorcycle accidents.

My father, who grew up experiencing the bomb shelters of Liverpool during the Second World War, was acutely aware of how fragile life is, and we had neighbors who had fled the war after witnessing atrocities, including the execution of their parents. My Uncle Steve spent the war in a Burmese prison camp. Everyone I was close to had experienced both real and potential threats. My dad's family once came home to an unexploded bomb on their front doorstep. For him it was a foundational training in never taking anything for granted.

But along with this existential anxiety in my family came a wicked sense of humor. My cousin Brian once suggested that the "two-man pallbear" should be an Olympic sport, and that our family might have our one shot at greatness in this category, since we were so practiced at pallbearing. My cousin Paul is the current (and likely forever) holder of the best funeral award, since he died "in the line of duty" as a firefighter and got a whole parade. On the day of the funeral, the rest of us cousins groused about what a show-off he was.

These days my address book looks redacted. I really should toss it out and start over, because so many pages are occupied by people now deceased. And always, when I think about the people I love, I wish that I really could stop time, so that I could hold on to them forever.

But no one wants to be the prisoner of someone else's neediness. That's what the fight against impermanence looks like. It's tight. It's fearful. It's grasping. None of us gets out of here alive. The part of us that knows we're impermanent is always in a battle with the part that wants to deny the passage of time and create a fortress of self to hide in. We take selfies, we tell stories, we buy lots of stuff, rack up all kinds of achievements—all attempts to make ourselves feel invincible and permanent and important—and to stop time, to stop aging, sickness, and death. But the reality is that the thing that makes us real is loving and being loved. Relationships are what make us real, and no matter how hard we try, no matter how good we are, we can't control the outcome. We still lose people we adore. Something much bigger is at play, and we are just a minuscule part of that big ineffable something.

The good news about impermanence is that every day is a new day, a new opportunity to be intimate with what is here now. We always have the possibility of redemption. The hard part is that we have to let go of our sense of self-importance, our sense that we are the center of the universe, and the belief that the world can't go on without us. We also have to believe that we can go on in the face of pain. The impulse to stop time doesn't come from a fear of death—it comes from a fear of life.

Practice & Reflect

Journal:

- Write about someone or something that you lost, whether through a breakup, a death, or just random circumstances.
- What stories did you tell yourself about what happened at the time?
- What feelings came up?
- How did you cope?
- How have your feelings about it changed over time? Has your understanding about what happened changed with time?

Everybody Hurts, Sometimes

The problem with being dissatisfied is not that you're dissatisfied; the problem is everything that you add on to it. I like to call this dukkha-dukkha, or suffering about suffering.
—Michael Stone

As our meditation practices develop and deepen, one of the characteristics we may notice is just how uncomfortable and dissatisfied we often feel. No matter how well things are going in our lives, underneath it all, most of us still feel so much wanting, often without even being clear on what we want. Or we may be plagued by anxiety, or regret, or disappointment. The Buddha had a word for this low-level but omnipresent suffering: he called it dukkha.

The word *dukkha* is as ancient as the ox-cart, and was used to describe the wear and tear of the wooden axel against the hub of the wheel, in the days before ball-bearings. The root *ka* means "space," and *du* means "dirty." This inevitable breakdown still occurs today, as anyone who's had a ride in my Hyundai can attest (ball joints wear out too; it just takes longer).

The Buddha's "first truth" was that all of us will have to deal with suffering. As self-aware creatures who cart around a sense of who we are based on our memories and experiences, and who also project ourselves into the future (because survival requires some planning), our sense of stability and safety is constantly coming into conflict with change.

When the change is outside of our control, as it often is, two factors lead to dukkha: our desire to hold fast to the things that bring us pleasure, and our desire to avoid the things that cause us pain. The Buddha did not say that life *is* suffering, but rather that dissatisfaction is the natural result of the contrast between our sense of security and the uncontrollable and ever-changing nature of reality. Having dukkha in our lives is as natural as having a tongue, or a liver, or a heartbeat. But although some unhappiness is inevitable from time to time, we can make our suffering better or worse according to how we respond to it.

Many psychotherapists and teachers differentiate pain from suffering in the following way:

- Pain is the result of physical distress or illness or unavoidable reaction to loss. When you chop your hand with a kitchen knife, you feel pain. When your dog gets run over, you feel pain.

- Suffering has more to do with how we react, how we talk about or think about the pain that has happened to us. Suffering is when you tell yourself how stupid you are for not paying attention while you were chopping, or how if your partner had only sharpened that knife like she promised, this wouldn't have happened. Suffering is the internal journey into habits of narrative and patterns of thinking that ensnare us. And often, suffering is the gap between how things actually are and how we think they *should* be.

Historically, psychologically, and culturally we all have a complicated relationship with pain and suffering, and every religion has its own take on what suffering is and what it means. Christians believe that the suffering that Jesus agreed to acted as atonement for the sins of humanity, and that his sacrifice would change the outcome of natural events. Many other religions expected sacrifices to appease the gods. The sacrifice required a person or an animal to suffer on behalf of others, which, if consciously entered, was an act of heroism.

I was raised in a rural area of Ontario in a community of Irish Catholics. My mother was a devout mix of Irish and Métis, and my father was from an Irish/English working-class family in Liverpool. If you know anything about old-fashioned Irish Catholics, you will know that suffering in Catholicism is an art form. If you've ever read Frank McCourt's wonderful memoir *Angela's Ashes,* you'll know the psyche he describes—and I can vouch for it. Martyrdom was much admired, and flagellation was sometimes part of the monastic tradition. The ultimate mark of Catholicism, the Catholic Olympic achievement, was to bleed spontaneously from the hands and the feet as a sign of compassion for Jesus—the mark of stigmata. Stigmata was the ultimate ability to take on the suffering of others and transform it.

In our narratives about the hero's journey (the archetypal foundation of most of our stories and movies), suffering is the litmus test of character. Overcoming obstacles and losses can become a measure of achievement and a source of pride. Have you ever heard the Monty Python skit in which two men argue back and forth about who had the hardest childhood? One says he walked five miles to school, and the other that he walked five miles too, only with no shoes, and on and on it goes, becoming ever more ridiculous. Sometimes we hang on to our suffering as a badge of honor. We believe that it makes us exceptional. And, of course, it can also be an excuse for our failings. Clearly, it may be a legitimate excuse, and by no means should the long-term effects of grief and trauma be downplayed. What's important is to distinguish between the pain of what actually happened and the pain embedded in our stories about what happened. We can't undo history, but we can rewrite our experiences in more empowering terms.

In our culture there is a persistent association between art and suffering. An idea that healthy, functional people don't make good art. So much the better if they are racked by addiction and out of control. Think of our obsession with celebrities like Whitney Houston and Amy Winehouse, and the schadenfreude—the perverse amusement—we derive from their predictable demises. We admire writers like Hemingway or Hunter S. Thompson for their ability to not conform, to refuse to function, but we only admire them because they had material accomplishments and celebrity. We do not admire the same behavior in our ex-brother-in-law or the homeless man who lives in the bus shelter. Pain, in the art world, is often viewed as fruitful. And think about the correlation between suffering and desire, pain and eros. No love story plot line is complete without the "boy loses girl" interlude. The drama, the character arc, demands a descent into chaos if the hero is to emerge triumphant.

Similarly we test ourselves against suffering. We prove ourselves by running marathons, by taking part in events that leave us blistered and exhausted. There is a part, in each and every one of us, and in our culture, that respects and elevates suffering. In fact, in some ways we have a currency of suffering. Suffering can give us credibility. It can feed our sense of individualism, our egotism, our sense of being unique.

Do you know anyone who habitually clings to suffering? I think we've all been guilty of it at some point or another, because a feeling of victimization can give us a powerful sense of purpose. One of my favorite literary examples is Dickens's Miss Havisham, who was abandoned at the altar and appears in *Great Expectations* twenty years later, still in her wedding dress, determined to take revenge on the male half of humanity. I've always had a begrudging admiration for Miss Havisham, because it takes a lot of energy and determination to stay mad for that length of time. But therein lies the pathos of her situation. She is so deep in the well of her suffering that she really can't see the rest of the world. She even stopped the clocks in the house on the day she was betrayed. Relationship is what eventually changes her. Once Miss Havisham finally sees the error of her ways, her horrid wedding dress catches on fire. She begs for forgiveness and, shortly thereafter, dies a stereotypical Dickensian death.

As an aside, investigators at the University of California have discovered that long-term or "stuck" grief activates neurons in the brain's reward centers that may prompt an addiction response. Those of us who cling to grief may be getting a form of perverse physiological pleasure. They named the condition "the Miss Havisham Effect."

We also have a legal system that can reward clinging to suffering. This is not a new development. Dickens wrote a book about it in 1853, *Bleak House*. The problem with legal suits that aim to collect compensation for pain and suffering is that the sufferer is prevented from moving on. Legal cases can linger on for years, and insurance companies spend considerable time and money making sure that they're not being bilked (and to be fair, they do contend with fraud and it ends up costing us all). But what it looks like on the ground is a person who's afraid to take out the garbage for fear that she'll lose her disability benefits while she's waiting for her case to be resolved in court (even though her fractures have healed, and she's capable of doing so). We create a lot of suffering through our ideas about justice, our ideas that we can balance crimes with punishments and that there is some mathematical way to even it all out. When we, or someone we love has been a victim of a crime, there is no jail sentence harsh enough to ease our suffering. The justice system doesn't have that kind of power.

We can make the mistake of grasping onto suffering, but we can also err in the opposite direction by imagining that we can eliminate it. We like to believe that if we have enough money, or enough friends, or enough power, we can avoid it. And in one sense this is true, because the privileged generally do suffer much less than most. But no matter how wealthy or powerful you are, you're still going to get old, and sick, and eventually die.

Our attempts at avoiding reality usually lead to more suffering. Many industries prey on our fear of mortality and also routinely point out the ways we're not living up to our potential. They poke pins into our existential worries about being successful enough, healthy enough, or attractive enough. They promise that the purchase of their product or service will take away the suffering of "not-enoughness" and then continually remind us of the ways that we fail to measure up. But no matter how much we buy, the dissatisfaction with the conditions of our lives will inexorably trickle back into our awareness, because it's built in to us.

Sadly, some of this storyline exists in the yoga community and the ways that yoga is marketed. The subtext is that yoga will make you youthful, more sexual, and more beautiful. You don't see many ads featuring yogis with cellulite or buck teeth. And according to the zeitgeist, good yogis should avoid the newspapers, because it creates negative energy. And we should avoid "negative" people, because they take us away from bliss. The cult of "positivity" within some yoga communities is just another way of refusing to acknowledge and deal with suffering in the world. There's value in choosing to be upbeat, but it's a choice that needs to be tempered with sensitivity and awareness toward those who *are* suffering.

We also need to beware of the belief we all have at some level that suffering is fair—that if we are good people, kind and compassionate, vegan, and helpful to others, suffering can be avoided. It can't. Beautiful, loving, joyful people get run down by trucks, blown up by terrorists, or stricken with cancer. Greedy, self-obsessed, nasty people get rewarded with wealth and reality shows. The division of the world into good and evil, right and wrong, black and white doesn't work. We know this intellectually, but we still harbor our child-like beliefs that some outside force, some celestial fairy godmother is going to come along and make it right. We think suffering is personal. We believe we're being punished or that there must be someone or something to blame. And that trap can keep us stuck for years, or cause us to strike out and hurt someone else.

Rather than trying to avoid suffering, this path asks us to normalize and attend to it. Pain and grief are inevitable—the work lies in acknowledging pain, caring for it with gentleness, and letting go of our tendencies to twist our suffering into a currency, a weapon, or a wall. Like a Chinese finger puzzle, the more we try to escape suffering, the tighter it binds us. Often the only way to escape pain is to stop trying to escape. As we develop more tools for coping and self-investigation, we can make space for the inevitable and universal ups and downs of being human. William Blake said, "Joy and woe are woven fine," and once we accept that they are two sides of a Möbius strip, we can move on to more important tasks: caring for each other, caring for the planet, and meeting each moment with attention and gratitude.

Practice & Reflect

Practice:

- Set timer for twenty minutes.
- Think about one situation or relationship that causes you pain.

Journal:

- For the first ten minutes, write down, in list form, the main stories you tell about it, e.g., "It's not fair," or "I'm being taken advantage of."
- For the next ten minutes, consider your list items in terms of whether they indicate clinging to something or being averse to something. For example: Do you hold fast to the idea that all relationships must be fair at all times?
- The point of this exercise is not to resolve anything, but rather to look deeper at the underlying assumptions beneath the discomfort.

Becoming More Flexible About Self-hood

Lo, I am with you always means when you look for God,
God is in the look of your eyes,
in the thought of looking, nearer to you than yourself,
or things that have happened to you.
There's no need to go outside.
Be melting snow.
Wash yourself of yourself.
— Rumi[2]

Here's a conundrum that I'm facing: when I think about writing a self-help book, what exactly is it that is being helped? Or in the vocabulary of millennials, how is it we can be our best self? And how do we find our true self of all the possible selves we could be, of all the possible selves we could become?

Partly this is a problem of language, because the concept of "self" in yoga means something different than the atomized, isolated self we talk about in the West. In the West we think of the self as made up of biology, history, our achievements, and social position—and our separateness and uniqueness are qualities to be built upon and clung to. So when, as Westerners, we talk about our true self, we are usually talking about some more ideal, improved (i.e., younger, thinner, wealthier, happier, more accomplished) imagined version of what we are now. We only need to quit our job/change our partner/move/lose ten pounds—and our true self will be revealed to *ooh*s and *ahh*s from our imaginary on-board audience. Chasing after this true self can be just one more road to suffering.

No one is suggesting that we should be without an ego.[3] To participate in the world, we need a fundamental sense of self, a sense of where our boundaries begin and end. But we get tripped up when we imagine our self to be a real, fixed, concrete entity, when in fact our selves are changing all the time.

Try this thought experiment: Imagine you can time-travel back to when you were sixteen years old, and that you kept a diary. Then imagine being asked to read it out loud, today, to your closest friends and family. (There was a radio show on CBC that asked people to actually do this, and it was hilarious.) Think back to who you admired, who you were in love with, your favorite items of clothing, and the ways you spent your time. Chances are, the person you are today is radically different from the person you were then.

At sixteen I was aging out of my love for Shaun Cassidy, and spent many of my leisure hours sneaking around drinking with friends and listening to "Jungle Love" by Van Halen. I hung out with all the wrong boys, including my drop-out boyfriend who, when I broke up with him, chased me around town with a rifle. I permed my hair, wore big shoulder pads and jeans I had to lie down to get into, and I could eat about 3,000 calories a day without gaining an ounce. I was active in my church, held a couple of part-time jobs, and had absolutely no idea what I wanted out of my life, or even that I had much control. I figured I'd get married, have a bunch of kids, and things would continue on much the way they always had. When I look back, I think: Who was that person?

The self, or the ego, is changing all the time, but we can't see the changes because of the point of view we occupy. Becoming aware of this creates a tremendous opportunity for freedom, and for changing direction, for growth, and for spontaneity.

The Buddhists have a term, *anatta*, sometimes translated as "egolessness," which could be described as an openness or willingness to be flexible about your identity. In its best manifestation it translates into curiosity, playfulness, and having a sense of humor. You still have a sense of self, but if your grandchild says, "Be a dog," you can actually loosen up enough to imagine how to be one. If you're diagnosed with a debilitating illness, having anatta means that you accept the person that you are becoming still deserves love and dignity. And if you lose your job, you can move on more easily, because your ideas about who you are aren't fixated on filling a certain role or making a certain income. Anatta is considered a "fact of life" that helps us not to cling to externals so much, and can help us escape the bombardment of a consumer culture that insists we should be fashionable, thin, forever young, blemish-free, and always busy.

There's a saying that "Yoga is a journey from the self, through the self, to the self." But in yoga there are two "selves": the small, isolated, egocentric self, and the grand, spacious, all-encompassing energy sometimes described as "the universe," or God. To call that "world-soul" the self at all is confusing, but the idea is that we are each a separate piece of this much larger entity and trying to reunite with it—trying to find our way home.

Buddhism is similar, but different. In Buddhism, self-hood is an illusion of language, a by-product of thinking, naming, and labeling. The self is not separate from the great world-soul. It never was, nor can it ever be, but experientially it *feels* separate. The challenge for Buddhists is to get past the ego and the limitations of imagination to wake up to the interconnectedness of all things. Dōgen says, "To study the self is to forget the self. To forget the self is to awaken to the 10,000 things" (i.e., everything).

Most Western religions believe in an immortal soul that moves on after we die. I hope that is true, but I really don't know. And like many people, I puzzle about what that would look like, and whether, if you had a leg amputated, you'd get it back in the afterlife. But regardless, the idea of inter-being and interconnection makes a lot of sense to me. I like the idea of the self having much looser boundaries—of a self that is always shifting and changing. In this view of the world, my true self includes everything and everyone, from the birds at the feeder to the cat trying to hunt them, from Nelson Mandela to the Boston Bomber.

Who we are, and who we can be is the result of an infinite number of conditions and circumstances, and every choice that we make changes the outcomes—as depicted in the movies *Groundhog Day* or *The Butterfly Effect*. There is no such thing as a "true self" or a "best self," because how could you ever be anything other than your true self? Unless you are an actor playing a role, you probably are being authentically you most of the time, and when you're faking it, you'll tire pretty quickly.

I'm not advocating complacency or laziness, or living out the rest of your days on your couch because you've achieved perfection. We could all afford to do better in our relationships with other beings and the world. But we can make these improvements from a place of love rather than fear. We can investigate the ways we are connected as opposed to always seeking to stand out. And usually the less we try to stand out, the more we will.

Practice & Reflect

Journal:

- Choose a time in your life at least ten years ago, or an age that you remember well. Answer the following:
- Who did you admire?
- What was your favorite TV show or movie?
- Who was your best friend?
- What expectations did you have for your future?
- What did you weigh?
- What did you like to wear?
- What were your passions or hobbies?
- Review your answers to the questions above.
- How many of them are still true for the "current" you?
- Can you remember what conditions or circumstances brought about the changes?

Feeling Groovy: Habit Patterns and Samskaras

Nothing so needs reforming as other people's habits.
— Mark Twain

If you think about it, what we are could be described as the sum of our habits. The ancient yogis noticed our propensity to get stuck in ruts and actually had a name for this cyclical behavior: they called our habit patterns *samskaras* (from which the English word "*scar*" originated). The good news is that we can cultivate new habits using the tools offered by our yoga and meditation practices. We can weed out the bad ones and replace them with new ones that will make us happier and healthier.

Yoga is all about identifying our habits. Obviously we have movement habits, which show up as areas of tightness or restriction in our bodies. We also have habitual ways of taking in information, thinking, rationalizing, dealing with feelings, and behaving.

Scientists who study habits have discovered that when we practice a skill routinely and regularly, it essentially becomes subconscious. Our habitual patterns are gradually "wired" into deeper, older brain structures (basal ganglia), where programs can run without us having to pay attention to them. This energy-saving brain function means we don't have to check the map every day before driving to the office. Once we have the route memorized, we don't have to use up critical decision-making energy. The first time I drove a car, the experience was exhausting for me and nerve-racking for my instructor. Now I can drive to my destination, listen to the radio, and plan a class in my mind all at the same time. Habits are efficient and operate in a fairly simple loop: cue—routine—reward.

When it comes to breaking habits or developing new ones, you would think the process easy—identify the cue, change the routine, and substitute a better reward. But if it were easy, the diet industry wouldn't be worth bezillions of dollars, and nobody would smoke. We're just not that simple.

Yoga psychology locates the cue at the sensory level. I have a feeling, I either like it or dislike it, and then the brain kicks in with suggestions about how to react and how to rationalize my reaction. In my case, whenever I feel anxious, I don't like feeling anxious, so my brain suggests going to check my email. I rationalize that choice by telling myself a story about missing out on something important. The distraction sidetracks my anxiety, until I actually read my email, and then decide to go make tea to combat the anxiety caused by my email. This loop can repeat itself all day, because the trigger (anxiety) that's causing the problem isn't getting addressed by any of my responses, and the reward (distraction) is part of the problem.

The ability to concentrate, calm down, and then focus the lens of the mind on the feelings that trigger our habits is the first step in helping us to change them. We have to slow down in order to investigate what emotions are driving us, and then make a plan to substitute a better behavior. We might not always act on our insights, depending on our energy level or other conditions of our lives, but at least we know that we have options. Once we have awareness, we can put in place all the other things that help us to change, such as intentions, social support, role models, or alternative rewards. Habits can take some time to reform, but with effort we are more than capable of changing them, and, by extension, the course of our lives.

Practice & Reflect

Journal:

- Think about a habit you would like to change, e.g., "I'd like to eat less fat."
- Identify the external triggers that cause the habit to happen. Think about the who, what, where, when, and why. If my spouse decides to have ice cream, for example, I want it too.

- Think about any internal sensations or feelings that trigger you. For example, when I watch the news in the evening, I feel agitated, so I want potato chips to distract me.
- Now make a list of possible solutions for each of the triggers. You could, for instance, ditch the spouse (I'm kidding).
- Come up with some things that might inspire you to change the habit, like a reward, a support team, or a reason why you need to make this change.

Hungry Ghosts

He who is contented is rich.
— Lao Tzu

As we ramble around our inner architecture, observing and investigating, it's inevitable that we'll run into some skeletons in our proverbial closets and ghosts in our psychological attics. In traditional tales, ghosts come to us with messages: a murder to be solved, a secret to be revealed, or a transgression to be avenged. Buddhist cultures have ghosts too, but they enter the ghost realm because of their own behavior during their time on earth—they become ghosts as a form of punishment.

The *gaki*, or "hungry ghosts," are usually depicted as human beings with huge bellies and freakishly tiny throats. Typically, they represent people who have been greedy and selfish in previous lives. The hungry ghosts have large appetites, but they are unable to eat. They can only consume enough to keep them alive, but not enough to find relief or satisfaction. Or in some iterations, they are able to eat, but every piece of food they touch turns into something disgusting (like blood or flesh), or inedible (like hot coals). The hungry ghosts represent our own inability to be satisfied. We have desires that we can never fulfill, and they usually have nothing to do with food. Often they're about security and safety, status, and ego, sometimes health or appearance or the need for attention. The insatiable need, whatever it is, is rooted in fear. We fear that we don't have enough money, resources, skills, Facebook-followers, time, clothes, degrees …you get the picture. We're so consumed by our fears that we fail to enjoy the bounty of things that are sitting here, right in front of us.

To exorcise our hungry ghosts, we have to digest the fact that something innate in us just cannot be satisfied. It's not necessarily our fault. We evolved to plan for contingencies, and we live in a culture that's all about having the biggest, the shiniest, and the best of everything. We really have to appreciate the presence of craving and understand its allure if we are ever going to loosen its grip. We can't let go of craving until we can see where it's turning up, just like in the movie *The Sixth Sense*—Cole has to acknowledge and talk to the ghosts that haunt him, in order to be left alone. Our hungry ghosts never totally leave us, but we can learn to live with them in peace. Craving is normal; our problem comes from pretending that it doesn't affect us.

Practice & Reflect

Journal:

- Set timer for ten minutes.
- Write down the question "What do I crave?"
- Jot down everything that comes into your mind in response to that question.
- Don't edit or analyze. Don't judge. Be honest.

After you're done, see if you can slot your answers into the following categories (from Maslow's hierarchy of needs):

- Physical or physiological
- Safety and control
- Love and belonging
- Self-esteem and competence
- Personal growth or creative expression

How Our Words Shape Who We Are

The limits of my language means the limits of my world.
— Ludwig Wittgenstein

I love reading, writing, and good conversation. I'm obsessed with language and the nuances of words, the power of a well-turned phrase, or the delight of an unexpected juxtaposition. I just about split a gut when my friend Gerald said he thought he might have some sunscreen in his "condiments pack," by which he meant his toiletries bag. But words come with limitations and baggage. Using a word to label something can diminish both the object we've labeled and our ability to perceive it fully. Once you learn the name of something, you never really experience it in the same way. You never see it with the same wonder or curiosity. Language simplifies the world on one hand (we have a tacit agreement about what constitutes a tree), but complicates it on the other (e.g., we use the word *love* in so many ways that effectively the term becomes meaningless). Language is a way of sorting and categorizing and making sense of things, but it can also result in our missing the details.

Have you ever loved two people in exactly the same way?

Patanjali says in the Yoga Sutra: "Word, meaning and perception tend to get lumped together, each confused with the others; focusing on the distinctions between them with perfect discipline yields insight into the language of all beings."[4] Our ability to understand, process, and create is literally dependent on our capacity for language, but at both ends of the spectrum. We need to grasp the intimacy, the enlightenment, and the luminosity that language can provide, and at the same time recognize when language is being weaponized to obfuscate, promote lies, or bully. George

Orwell's dystopian novel *1984* was a case study in how dumbing down language could dumb down a population and render it more controllable. The less vocabulary a person can access, the less their capacity to reason verbally. Dictators and miscreants of all stripes usually go on the attack against education (the source of word-power), and those who've been educated—not the bureaucrats (they always survive) but the thinkers, the creatives, the poets, and the philosophers.

But written languages are not the only languages. We are surrounded by languages we aren't even aware of: like the ultrasonic conversations between rats and the singing of mice,[5] or the chemically mediated communications that happen between trees. Language is multiple, varied, multisensory (think body language, sign language) and contextual.

We often fail to appreciate the presence or the power of language. Language drives behavior, and it can be constructive or destructive. Only when we stop speaking and listen to our internal chatter can we truly appreciate how language creates us at the same time as we're creating it.

Practice & Reflect

Journal:

- Make a list of the languages you know, e.g., English, French, poetic, mathematic, symbolic, body language.
- Which of these languages comes to you most easily? Why?
- Do you use different languages in different relationships (e.g., with your parents versus with your friends)?

What's Going on with My Energy?: The Three Gunas

My get up and go has got up and went.
— Homer A. Shiveley

As we become more skilled at investigating our minds and bodies, we can try on different worldviews for the insights that they give us. The yogis believed that the world is made up of creative energy (not so different from what physicists tell us today), and that this energy is a braiding together of three different sub-types known as the *gunas*.

The word *guna* means "string, thread or strand," and the three gunas are eternal and present in everything and everyone. Constantly shifting and changing according to our choices and habits, one can become dominant. This model presents an interesting lens for viewing our experiences, perceptions, and moods as we dance with changes in our daily lives.

The three gunas map very well onto what we know about the human nervous system, although it would be unfair and reductive to say that this model is restricted to the human experience. The gunas go beyond the boundaries of any particular organism and are part of everything, including natural cycles (birth, reproduction, death), the foods we consume, and our relationships.

Sattva is the guna associated with harmony, intelligence, and happiness. In relationship to the nervous system it would equate to a parasympathetic state, where we feel relaxed, rested, and at ease. *Rajas* is the energy of passion, activity, and desire. It might be likened to the sympathetic nervous system and the energy of stimulation—fight or flight. *Tamas* is a state of dullness, inertia, or illusion. Current nervous system theory would describe this state as "dorsal," or immobilized. Energetically this state may present as numbness, detachment, or dissociation.

Although in theory we'd like to exist in a sattvic state all the time, the gunas don't work that way. Rather, we shift from one guna to another, depending on our tendencies, our genetic make-up, and the circumstances that surround us. Energetically, we have to adapt and deal with this impermanence—it's not always within our control.

Sometimes the gunas are described in the context of time and the way our lives are unfolding. Tamas represents the past and the lot we've been given; it's already been determined without our agency. Rajas could be considered a drive toward the future, and includes desire, projection, anticipation, or fear. Sattva is positioned in the middle, and represents the present moment, which is the only place where we can make change. Ideally, as yogis we want to expand our time in sattva.

Our energy levels are always evolving. When life is going well and we're in a sattvic state, we exercise, eat well, and are fun to be around. But then something will change. We might get sick, or lose our job, or maybe we just get bored. We stop attending our program at the gym, drink more than we should, surrender to our cravings, and gain a few pounds. We feel lethargic, dull, and unmotivated. We need to rest and withdraw. This tamasic state will go on for a few days, months, or years, until we realize we've had enough of it. Then a rajasic period begins: we take up a new hobby, buy some new clothes, and sign up for a dozen events. We tend to act impulsively and passionately without thinking things through. We might get ourselves into a rebound relationship, take on too much work, or spend more than we can afford. We start to get worried, irritable, and caffeine-reliant. If we have the insight to see that we've become rajasic, we might be able to down-shift to a more balanced sattvic state, but if not, we end up crashing back to tamas.

Wherever we end up, it's only a phase. As we get better at noticing and attending to our interior landscape, we can manage these energies more skillfully and spend more time in sattva. But grasping after sattva can also be folly, because the true nature of our experience is change. As Richard Freeman explains, "Either you will wind up rajasic in your pursuit of sattva or you will become upset at the inevitable decay of your sattvic state into a sleepy, dull, fixed, tamasic state."[6]

Using this model can help us better understand our psychological tendencies and recognize that ups and downs are inevitable. As we observe our energy shifts, greater awareness can help us make better choices. For example, when we're in a rajasic period, we know that we should consult a friend before signing up for more online training, or think twice about taking on a new contract that we don't have adequate time to fulfill. When we're in a tamasic state, we can look for motivation and support, and perhaps sign up for Weight Watchers again. We can see the impermanence and even the humor in our tendencies, and that insight alone will help us spend more time in that sattvic, happy middle ground.

Practice & Reflect

Journal:

- Which guna do you generally lean toward?
- Can you identify a time in your life that was particularly tamasic?
- Can you also remember a rajasic period?
- What three activities might help you move toward finding more balance (sattva)?

Echoes of Narcissus

They say that the road to hell is paved with good intentions, which was really where the problems of Narcissus began. Had he not been so arrogant, so full of disdain for the people who loved him, Nemesis would most certainly have left him to his own devices. She would have admired his beauty, like so many others, and rejoiced in his exceptional luck; because not many of us are born outwardly beautiful, and those who are beautiful are accorded slightly more worth than those who are not. It has always been this way.

But Narcissus was full of scorn, and Nemesis, feeling the need to teach him a lesson, used her powers to attract him to a stagnant pool, where upon seeing his reflection he became transfixed. He fell in love with his own image, and was so entranced that eventually he wasted away, and as the story goes, transmogrified into the flower that bears his name.

But about this part, the Greeks were mistaken. When Narcissus pined away to nothing, he did not turn into a flower. The flower had been growing there for many years, in spite of being frequently trod upon by our handsome antihero, and when Narcissus slipped down into the shallows, it was the flower who watched the last traces of his final exhale bubble to the surface. But flowers know that their time is fleeting, and soon enough it lifted its gaze and turned its attention to better things.

Narcissus had fallen into a ponderous trap, clinging devotedly to a mistaken object. Had it not been his own reflection, we would be talking of him with sympathy, for who among us has not fallen in love with someone unattainable? The sad truth for Narcissus is that he never gained the ability to see himself. Nemesis thought that was the end of it, not realizing that in punishing Narcissus so cruelly, she had allowed him to enter into a completely different cycle of existence; one that reiterated itself over and over again. For Narcissus is very much alive and well, and his arrogance and hubris are traits that lately we seem quite inclined to reward, particularly in corporate finance and the exploitation of natural resources. So we mustn't think too harshly of him.

But this story is not really about him. It is about Echo, who fell hopelessly and deeply in love with Narcissus.

Echo was overcome by his beauty, and really believed, in her heart of hearts, that he could change—if only he had the love and devotion of his true soul-mate; a woman who could delve into his depths and nurture the wounded child below the surface. Echo was deluded, but she was a product of the myths and fairy tales she had been immersed in as a child. So Echo spent endless hours crouched in the cattails, watching Narcissus watching himself. She had no ability to plead with him, having lost the power of self-expression because of Hera's curse. She could only repeat the last few words he spoke to her, which were something to the effect of "You're attractive for a mountain nymph, but that's just not enough." And so her protestations were mute, which suited Narcissus absolutely. In the tradition of romantic self-destruction, she withdrew and gradually pined away, until nothing but her voice remained.

When Narcissus succumbed to his fate and slipped down into the pool, what remained of Echo dove in after him. But as he entered the water a most curious thing took place. As his earthly body disintegrated, the essence of him returned to the water—we are all, after all, mostly just water—and the water gave him a new form of existence. Like Echo, he was disembodied but continued to exist as a damp, permeable, and expanding ghost, lacking the boundaries of skin and the burdensome weight of bone. As he grew accustomed to his new form of consciousness, his pride began to grow anew. Through the passage of time and cycles of precipitation he grew, gradually becoming aware and more sentient. Until he began again to seek the beautiful young man he remembered from his past life.

Echo, who had taken hope that Narcissus, now disembodied too, would finally see the suitability of their relationship, remained alongside him. She loved him still, and deeply, in spite of his selfishness and complete emotional unavailability, and she pursued him through brook and stream, puddle and rivulet, river and rapid. But still he spurned her, telling her, "You are not enough." And helplessly she repeated, "Not enough, not enough, not enough." Her unencumbered tears simply made their way back to the ocean.

Eventually his essence grew and spread, infiltrating the reservoirs and underground streams, and contaminating the water that gives all of us life. Absorbed in stages and parts-per-million he entered the bodies of millions of us, by virtue of osmosis. Still he longed for the unattainable, chasing a never-ending sense of dissatisfaction, but that longing is now shared by the human organisms that host him. Narcissus has become a parasite. And Narcissus is still drawn to mirrors, and to searching for the one thing he can never possess, because, tragically, he never didn't have it. And Echo is still bound to him, whispering, "Not enough, not enough, not enough."

Unhappily-ever-after these two will be enmeshed, in a perverse and tragic marriage, in an unbreakable bond. They have inadvertently spawned an entire industry. We have absorbed them both like the countless containers of skin-cream-promises and cosmeceuticals that clutter our bathroom cabinets and vanities. And when our attempts to stifle them fail, we inject a little botulism around our eyes and collagen in the corners of our mouth, and stand transfixed before mirrors that whisper "Not enough, not enough, not enough." We have no time or inclination now, to revel in the beauty of the spring flower that managed to thrive in the absence of Narcissus.

The Secret Power of the Stories We Tell

The world is like the impression left by the telling of a story.
— Yogavasistha, 2.3.11

When I was a kid, I got teased a lot about how I looked. I was scrawny, gangly, and had bad teeth. My sister nicknamed me "Frankenberry," (after the Frankenstein monster who was the mascot for a breakfast cereal) and when my hair was cut short, I was constantly mistaken for a boy. Needless to say, I never related much to Cinderella or any of the Disney heroines. My favorite fictional character was an undersea witch. Even later, when in retrospect I realized I wasn't that ugly, the story got in my way for decades, and I made some terrible decisions because of it. Ironically, once I'd decided that my true gift must be my intellect, I was bullied at school for being too smart. After a few years of enduring the nickname "Elaine-the-brain," I stopped putting my hand up in class. The safest thing, I thought, was to say nothing, stay out of the public eye, and blend in as much as possible. I made up this story based on scant and misperceived evidence, but it held me back. Just because stories are factually untrue doesn't make them less powerful emotionally. When I came across Amy Farrah Fowler on *The Big Bang Theory* years later, I thought, "Finally, someone I relate to."

Over the years, I've recognized that some of the stories I invested in deeply, the stories that I used to define who I am, are no longer useful or particularly true. But they are really hard to let go of. Our stories can keep us stuck, because they make us feel safe, and we've grown comfortable with them. Often, even when the doors of insight are opened, we'll choose to stay put rather than take a risk on the unknown.

Where does our sense of being a "me," or a "self" come from? Is it innate? Inherited? Learned? If you asked the scientific community to weigh in, the answer would undoubtedly be all of the above. Some of our temperamental traits are evident at birth, others come with our experiences, and still others come from the way we *choose* to tell our stories, both inwardly and outwardly.

We humans tell stories to make sense of our world both consciously and unconsciously. Much of our learning in early childhood is woven into the form of fairy tales, storybooks, and Hollywood movies. We learn our morality based on what happened to the evil stepsisters or selfish giant. We gain a sense of our family through the anecdotes told to us by our parents and grandparents. Underneath every choice, every opinion, and every intention is some kind of narrative.

Even as we busily absorb stories from the outside, we're also weaving our own narratives to make sense of our experiences, and the times we are living through. But as the authors of our own stories, we have to recognize that we are not faultless narrators. Research has proven that our memories are fluid and unreliable; just ask your siblings about an incident in your childhood, and you're likely to hear remarkably different versions of the event.

Our stories about who we are come from a point of reference that we can't really see. And our reference point is always changing. Our chief narrator is moody, a trickster, and a Scheherazade. Our new experiences tend to overwrite our old ones. When I was twenty-four I imagined that I'd fallen in love with my soul-mate. When I was thirty-two and going through my divorce, I imagined I'd married a monster. But with time and distance I can see that neither of these stories had any intrinsic truth. They were just parking spaces on a psychological journey.

We often tell stories in the form of gossip, which can be completely untrue. We wound with words, and are wounded by words. Injuries inflicted by sticks and stones are visible and easily patched up. Words can inflict damage that is unseen and long-lasting.

The stories we tell ourselves can be of our own creation, but they comprise many threads not of our own making. Some of the pieces may be archetypal, or from popular culture like movies or media. We can hold competing stories in our minds that are both true, such as the tale of the ant and the grasshopper that is reimagined in the movie *Ferris Bueller's Day Off*. The ant character models working hard and creating security; the grasshopper's character is about stepping out of routine and seizing the moment. Both aims are admirable, it all depends on the situation.

Stories can be deeply intertwined with power and politics. As is often the case, those who cannot be heard, or who cannot tell their own stories, will have their stories told by others, usually to great disadvantage. Much of the history of Indigenous peoples in North America has been based on fabrications, while a great deal that is unflattering to the early settlers of our nations has not been told.[7]

Reading fiction is a powerful way to create listening and empathy. Many years ago I was deeply moved by John Irving's novel *The Cider House Rules*. I started the novel an ardent anti-abortionist, and finished it with a much more nuanced view based on scenarios that I had never imagined. Reading fiction allows us to try on other people's viewpoints in a way that is much less threatening than, say, a political debate. When moving from the general to the particular in this way, we can imagine real humans rather than categories of people. We can see what I share with "not I."

Ursula Le Guin made the argument that storytelling can be the basis of change, that it's the first step on the path away from "the lazy, timorous habit of thinking that the way we live now is the only way people can live. It is that inertia that allows the institutions of injustice to continue unquestioned."[8]

Marketers are always trying to sell us "better stories," and there is nothing wrong with this once we have the insight to see the motivation behind it. When we can name a story for what it is, it loses a great deal of its power; it becomes a servant rather than a master.

Stories are the way we connect with one another, the way we build empathy, community, and relationship. Stories connect us to the past, and allow us to imagine and build our future. What meditation practice can do is allow us to find a more visceral truth. A truth that is *written on the body*, to steal a phrase from Jeanette Winterson. Practice can allow us to explore our treasured stories without the ego-mind jumping in to try to validate or invalidate them. With time we can distance ourselves enough to loosen up the hold that a story has, and we can choose to re-write and re-imagine it. Better endings are almost always possible.

Practice & Reflect

Journal:

- Make a list of three favorite novels, short stories, or movies.
- Identify what it was within these stories that resonated with you.
- Did they change your thinking? Did they clarify something?
- How did they make you feel?

Hearing Impaired

Can one put aside all these screens through which we listen, and really listen?
— Jiddu Krishnamurti

Once, when I was working as a home-care therapist in rural Ontario, I was asked if I could do anything for an elderly man who was living in a trailer on his son's farm. The nurses who visited him regularly were alarmed by the method that he was using to get up from the couch and down again, and were convinced he would have a bad fall.

When I met the man (let's call him George—not his real name, of course), it was clear that he pretty much lived on the chesterfield, and the cushions formed a silhouette of his body whether he was on it or not. The couch was circa 1968 and covered in a green, orange, and brown floral print. When I asked him to show me how he got up, he rolled from his reclined position down to the floor, and then used an adjacent La-Z-Boy (with the footrest extended) to crawl his way up to standing. I could see why the nurses were alarmed.

Excited that this was a problem I could solve, I went out to my car and came back with a set of wooden furniture raisers: four-inch blocks that increase the height of a sofa to make it easier to stand up from. I had quite a time lifting the couch on my own to get them in, but I'm pretty determined, and I got 'er done. We practiced going from sitting to standing a few times and then made a date for my next visit.

The next week I went back expecting praise and thanks but was greeted by a very angry man. I found him in his usual position on the couch, and his first words to me were "Get these #@$%ing things out of here. They hurt!"

Confused, I asked him to show me. He rolled from the couch (which was now four inches higher) and climbed up the La-Z-Boy the way he'd always done it. I didn't know whether to laugh or cry, but it was apparent that he was done with me and my fancy contraptions.

All this to illustrate the point that listening happens at many levels: physical (ears, eyes, body language, attention), psychological (willingness, trust, openness, habits), and spiritual (where we investigate our relationship to change, mortality, and meaning). I didn't really "see" George other than as a problem that needed solving. He couldn't "hear" me because of the force of his habits, his failing memory, and likely his ideas about female know-it-alls.

We live in a culture obsessed with talking and broadcasting. We all want what we want, and we have a cultural story about ourselves as isolated units competing in an economy of scarcity. We haven't been interested in listening to Nature, or science, or other spiritual and philosophical traditions, or Indigenous knowledges. In the last few years we've become shockingly divided and confused by the internet—which has joyous benefits, but no conscience or mechanism for filtering truths from fictions. And human beings are wired to have a confirmation bias: even if we know what we're reading is probably untrue, we'll believe it because it jibes with what we already "know." And of late, hyper-partisan politics (and social media) have made a mockery of communication altogether, leaving us with little capacity for problem solving or creative thinking. I can't think of another time in history where we've been more in need of real fact-based communication and a willingness to cooperate to solve extinction-level problems.

We're all experts at speaking, but we have a lot to learn about listening. Listening requires effort, tenacity, and acceptance of discomfort—because sometimes we have to endure hearing things we'd rather not know. It requires cleaning our interior slates long enough to absorb what's being communicated. We have to bracket our favorite opinions and resistance based on our past experiences and prejudices. This is really, really hard to do (and I fail at it frequently). Meditation helps. Body awareness helps. Having a community and the support of friends also helps.

Listening is about more than the words being spoken. At the sangha where I practice, we partake in partner discussions where one person speaks and the other just listens. It's intimate, anxiety-provoking, and incredibly useful. I can't think of anything quite so satisfying as feeling fully seen and heard. But it's not for the faint of heart. It requires a high level of openness, vulnerability, and trust. We also have some rules about respecting confidentiality, speaking honestly, and avoiding cross-talk (talking about what other people have shared when they don't have the opportunity to respond). It feels unnatural at first, but we've had some insightful, viewpoint-altering conversations.

Fully listening involves being able to attend to things in two directions at once: what is external to us, and what is going on inside (thoughts, moods, preferences). When we are able to attend to both, simultaneously, with curiosity and a sense of humor, we're practicing advanced yoga. Handstands are for beginners.

The Buddhist teacher Thich Nhat Hahn developed a written manifesto for his community called *The Fourteen Mindfulness Trainings*.[9] The first of these is Openness:

> Aware of the suffering created by fanaticism and intolerance, we are determined not to be idolatrous about or bound to any doctrine, theory, or ideology, even Buddhist ones. We are committed to seeing the Buddhist teachings as guiding means that help us develop our understanding and compassion. They are not doctrines to fight, kill, or die for. We understand that fanaticism in its many forms is the result of perceiving things in a dualistic and discriminative manner. We will train ourselves to look at everything with openness and the insight of interbeing in order to transform dogmatism and violence in ourselves and in the world.

In the face of global inequity, climate change, and a whole host of other societal problems, we need to be open to listening as well as speaking if we're ever going to change anything. It may feel impossible, but we can affect change within our own hearts and minds. It's a good place to start.

Practice & Reflect

The Buddhist teacher Martine Batchelor often teaches a type of listening practice I've found enlightening. Rather than making the object of meditation the breath, the object is a question, "*What is this?*"

- Set the timer for fifteen minutes.
- Sit, take some time to be calm and focused, and then drop the question "*What is this?*" into your mind.
- Here's the catch: *Do not answer the question.* Just keep asking it, over and over, like a mantra.
- Once you get the hang of it, you can continue asking yourself the question as you go about your regular routine.
- The first time I tried this meditation I thought I'd go out of my mind—as in insane, not in the desirable Zen sense of the phrase. After a lifetime of being trained to provide answers and expertise in school and my career, not answering felt like holding my breath. It screwed up my ideas about who I was—a seeker, a learner, a person-who-knows. It took a while to recognize how radically wise this practice is, and how it promotes listening and receiving.

And Out of the Darkness Came the Light

> *If you know someone who is depressed, please resolve never to ask them why: Depression isn't a straightforward response to a bad situation; depression just is, like the weather.*
> — Stephen Fry

The other day I was wasting time on Facebook and came across one of those games where you create a name for yourself based on random pairings of words and personal data. Due to my first initial and month of birth I was awarded the title Empress of the Frozen Darkness. This gave me pause.

When we start a committed meditation practice, and begin to investigate mind states, we enter the territory of emotions and moods. It's not uncommon, either, to have turned to yoga because we're trying to overcome emotional suffering. Emotions might be described as the combination of a bodily sensation and our story about what that sensation means. Moods tend to last longer, feel more pervasive, and have less connection to what's happening moment to moment and more to physiological factors like fatigue, light-levels, or hormones.

As we become more curious investigators, we may also become aware of increased levels of sadness or fear. We typically manage these emotions by being so busy, harried, or distracted that we don't have to deal with them. Those who have the means may turn to counselors or psychotherapists. Meditation is useful in helping us to identify, connect with and "feel the feels," but it's not a substitute for therapy or support from other humans. Becoming more in touch with our emotions can be a painful, uncomfortable process.

When I read the name Empress of Frozen Darkness, the mood state that popped into my head was depression. I have suffered from mild depression in the past; my brother and my mother have experienced periods of debilitating depression, and other members of my family (both my blood family and my friend family) are dealing with depression and anxiety right now. Frozen darkness struck me as an apt metaphor.

Depression is poorly understood by people who've never experienced it, and unfortunately we often use the word *depressed* to describe trivial mood states (e.g., I was depressed that I missed the season finale of *Stranger Things*). Being clinically depressed is not equivalent to feeling blue, being stuck in a bad mood, or needing an attitude adjustment. Those who advocate quick fixes or promises of easy relief through yoga, dietary changes, or self-help books are practicing a cruel form of disrespect.

The experience of depression can range from a pervasive sadness and lack of energy, to insomnia, frenetic activity, and panic (anxiety), to a feeling of being absolutely leaden and incapable of any sort of feeling at all. Depression can span a huge range of mental and bodily experiences, and often requires medical help to overcome. Yoga and meditation may help, but they are not likely to cure it; and in some cases, meditation may make severe depression worse.

Although the stigma of mental illness is not nearly as pronounced as it used to be, we have a long way to go in educating ourselves about depression, helping each other through it, and addressing erroneous attitudes and views about how it should be treated. In my experience, the fight to overcome depression requires a multifaceted approach, excellent social support, time, patience, and a good sense of humor. Some of us never overcome it. We learn to make space for it and continue on living in the best way that we can manage.

Most of the depressives I know are amazing people, so I guess I needn't feel so bad about being the Empress of Frozen Darkness. To quote the inimitable Arlo Guthrie, "You can't have a light without a dark to stick it in."

Practice & Reflect

Reach Out:

- Do you suffer from depression or know someone who does?
- Make a list of three to five local resources, such as psychotherapists, in your area (especially important if you teach yoga or work with people).
- Are there any local resources or outreach services you can support (e.g., with donations, or as a volunteer)?

Part Four:
Virya: What Do I Stand For?

> *Courage is the most important of the virtues, because without courage you can't practice any other virtue consistently. You can practice any virtue erratically, but nothing consistently without courage.*
> — Maya Angelou

Concentration, mindfulness, and investigation are skills that reveal and recreate our inner worlds. Like getting a new pair of prescription lenses, with them we see things more clearly, but it can be disorienting at first. Some of what we see is pleasing, and some is sad, difficult, or frightening. At this point in the yoga and mindfulness journey, the going gets harder. My teacher Michael used to say that this stage is when many people switch to Cross-Fit.

Virya is a Sanskrit word that connotes strength and manliness. Closely related to the word *virile*, it is also the namesake of a great warrior in the *Mahabharata*.[1] The question we must ask at this stage in our journey is "What do I stand for?" Virya requires that we make choices, and move beyond our selves out into the world—from investigation to action. This is the stage where we develop courage, perseverance, and enthusiasm.

When we're new to yoga, or any discipline, there's usually a honeymoon phase, a mastery phase, disillusionment, and then a "dry place."[2] If we're on the path for the long haul, we'll visit these stages more than once. Virya is required to keep putting one foot in front of the other, and it applies to all the projects and purposes in our lives. To get back up after a failure requires virya. To start over after a break-up requires virya. To stand up for the environment, or against hatred and oppression requires virya. Perseverance matters. Anything worthwhile requires determination and faith that the journey is worth completing. Virya is about overcoming both internal and external obstacles.

Our tasks in this stage of the journey are to make choices, act ethically, and take responsibility for our actions. Virya means showing up with an appropriate response to ever-changing situations even when we are afraid and uncomfortable. We feel the fear, and then we keep going. Like the postural yoga practice we're familiar with, working with virya builds a strong and supple spine.

Practice & Reflect

Journal:

- Make a list of three people you find inspiring.
- What admirable qualities do they embody?
- Are they courageous, and if so, how?

Karma and Consequences: We Are What We Do

We do not see things as they are. We see them as we are.
— Anaïs Nin

The way we talk about karma in our culture is often summed up as a theory of poetic justice. We like to think that the angry customer abusing the staff at the motor vehicles office is going to get a flat tire on her way home. In ancient India, karma related to ideas about reincarnation—those who lived moral lives and worked hard within their designated stations would be reborn into a better status, the highest status of all to be male and a member of the Brahmin, or "priestly," caste.

But in the Buddha's teachings, the word *karma* simply means to do, to act, or to create. Everything that we think, say, or do is an action, and our actions *are* our creations. How we act matters.

But, you say, I'm only one of seven billion individuals. In the big picture, I'm a grain of sand, a momentary blip in time and space. This is true and also not true. The reason your actions matter is that you're not alone here. You are part of a vast ecological web.

A story in the *Avatamsaka Sutta* tells of a magical net created by the god Indra. The net stretches infinitely in all directions and strings together the whole universe. At each junction is a mirrored, multifaceted jewel, and each jewel reflects every other jewel. Each one can be seen as the center of the universe, and at the same time the whole universe can be found within each jewel. The jewel represents you, and any time a corner of the net is moved, the ripples affect the entire universe. The net is held together by the threads of relationship: there is nothing in the entire web that isn't connected with an infinite number of other things.

In this view of the universe, we are not isolated individuals building up our status with perfect abs or the latest iPhone. There is no outside or inside, and no supreme point of view. We're not being graded or judged, and we're all being held in a boundless and incomprehensible network of relationships. When we pull on the threads, the effect is felt by those around us.

Karma behaves much like gravity. We're producing it, and experiencing it without necessarily being aware of it. Whenever we act physically, there are effects. When we drive distracted and accidentally kill someone, we can consider that karma. When we speak unkindly, there are effects—both for the victim of our comments and in the way we are viewed by others.

We also have habits of thinking that create karma. When we get stuck in habitual and mindless patterns, this cycle becomes steeped in suffering. For example, we've all known people who've divorced one spouse only to remarry another who's virtually indistinguishable from the first. The familiar feelings that this person engenders in them are mistaken for true love as opposed to what they really are, which is more of the same dysfunction they're accustomed to.

The problems originate in thinking and storytelling. When something new enters our universe through the gateways of our senses, there's an almost immediate tendency to react with either like or dislike, clinging or aversion. We justify our reaction with storytelling and egotism. In microseconds we may decide that we dislike someone based entirely on the way they look, where they live, or who they voted for in the last election. Based on our stories, we take action, and our actions either change us or drive us deeper into our habitual ruts. Our actions may lead to conflict and misunderstandings, or to the start of a new relationship. We can build diversity, or we can build walls. Either way, it's karma.

Our dispositions toward certain emotions and narratives create cycles. We may be disposed toward anger, and when we complain and growl at people, our life provides us more to be angry about. We tend to attract what we dish out, and perpetuate cycles of emotion and behavior. As Andrew Olendzki says, "Which wolf gets fed wins the day."[3]

Our actions in the present moment are creating our future life. And the stories and emotions that influence our actions are derived from our own past experiences. We're always creating and recreating ourselves, and if our intentions are to do better, to be kinder, and to be more loving, we are capable of doing that. Of course, this is complicated by the relationships we are in, and what other people are doing. We have no real control over our political leaders, or even the people we love the most. The only option we have is to roll with the punches, and take the time to respond, when we can, with wisdom.

Worrying about the consequences of every decision we make can become paralyzing, because nobody can predict the future. In the yoga text *The Bhagavad-Gita*, the main character, Arjuna, is a warrior struggling with the decision of whether or not to go into battle. He is tempted to do nothing, because he knows that any action he takes will lead to suffering. His companion, who is the god Krishna in disguise, explains to him that we all have to do our duty. We have to do the best that we know how to do. We take action, fully aware that we can never foresee all the consequences, and then we let go of the results. We wait to see what happens and correct our course accordingly. When you're not sure what to do, *try something*. It may not turn out the way you expected, but it's of more value than sitting and wringing your hands.

Yoga teacher Richard Freeman says, "The true mystery of life and of the present moment is revealed only through surrender, through letting go, through not controlling and not knowing."[4] This is not to say that we don't act, or that we do nothing. Rather we act without expectation of results, and we're awake to the fact that our actions do matter, because we're tied to everything and everyone in the net.

Recognizing the depth and breadth of our power to act, and recognizing our responsibility to minimize harmful consequences, we can dive into the practice of ethics with the innate understanding that the exercise will prepare us for what happens on the battlefield, or in the lunchroom at work.

Practice & Reflect

Before we move deeper into yoga ethics, it's helpful to explore the values or aspirations that drive our current behavior:

- Choose *one* value from the table below that is paramount for you. (It's awful having to pick just one, but do it anyway).

Journal:
- Set timer for fifteen minutes.
- Write down what value you chose as your #1.
- Write your ideas (and/or stories) about why you made this choice.

Achievement	Adventure	Authenticity	Boldness
Challenge	Compassion	Community	Contentment
Courage	Curiosity	Creativity	Environment
Ethics	Fairness	Faith	Fame
Family	Friendship	Fun	Generosity
Growth	Happiness	Honesty	Independence
Justice	Kindness	Learning	Meaningful Work
Openness	Optimism	Peace	Pleasure
Power	Responsibility	Respect	Recognition
Safety	Service	Simplicity	Success
Trustworthiness	Wisdom	Add your own if you don't see it here.	

Yoga Ethics: The Yamas and the Niyamas

> *There are different kinds of happiness, and the deep happiness of well-being comes from caring for yourself and loving the world. It comes from offering what's good in you to others, giving your gifts to a world that needs it. These kinds of happiness are the important kinds— the happiness of generosity, the happiness of your own integrity, and the happiness of an inner well-being that comes from tending the mind and heart so that what's beautiful in you can come forth.[5]*
> — Jack Kornfield

From the time we began living in communities to the present day, humans have had to deal with the constant tension of balancing what is good and healthy for ourselves against what is good and healthy for others. Freud wrote a book about this dilemma called *Civilization and Its Discontents*. He argued that to enjoy the benefits of living in a civilized society, we have to give up a measure of freedom, which a part of our personality usually resents.

The two polarities of caring for the self and caring for others do not necessarily contradict one another. In fact, societies that look after their poor and sick have lower rates of crime and greater overall happiness. Caring for others has well-documented psychological benefits.

The early teachers of Buddhism emphasized practice for personal liberation, but as the teachings spread, they shifted into what is known as Mahayana Buddhism, or the "greater vehicle." The Mahayana belief was that as long as others are suffering, no one can be completely free. No one can ever truly be an "outsider," because there is no outside in a world where everything is interconnected.

The traditional yoga teachings contained two "limbs" of practice meant to provide guidance about this balance. The first limb, known as the "yamas," comprises recommendations about "playing well with others." The five yamas are secular and can overlay most other spiritual systems without conflict:

AHIMSA	not harming
ASTEYA	not taking anything that is not offered (not stealing)
SATYA	honesty
APARIGRAHA	not taking more than you need, not being greedy
BRAHMACHARYA	the wise use of sexual energy

The niyamas are self-care or self-directed practices, and there are also five of these:

SAUCA	cleanliness/hygiene and discretion about what is taken into the body and mind
SANTOSHA	the cultivation of contentment
TAPAS	the drive to create and work and *do* things; self-discipline
SVADYAYA	self-study, education, enrichment, learning
ISHVARA PRANIDANA	the ability to surrender, to let go of control, to trust in a wisdom that transcends the ego

The last three niyamas grouped together are described as Kriya yoga, and operate like the Serenity Prayer:

God grant me the serenity to accept the things I cannot change, (Ishvara Pranidana)
Courage to change the things I can, (Tapas)
And the wisdom to know the difference. (Svadyaya)

The yamas are helpful when we seek a touchstone for integrity and generosity, and the niyamas reflect the care and attention to inner life that is needed to live with more ease and joy.

Guiding principles like the yamas and niyamas are useful tools, but there is nothing simple about enacting and embodying a stricture like "not-harming." On the whole you'll find the yamas and niyamas are principles to aspire to and a useful compass for times when we feel lost and uncertain. We'll often fail to live up to them, but they are meant to be aspirational, not another stick to beat ourselves up with.

Traditionally you wouldn't even start a classical yoga practice until you had a good handle on the ethical limbs, and had made peace with your parents. In later "Hatha" practices (developed hundreds of years after classical yoga), these limbs were not taught until many other practices were mastered, because they considered them too hard for beginners. These days many of us come to yoga hoping to escape from situations or jobs that take us out of our integrity. I think that's why so many people are anxious to become yoga teachers. Many of us flee the corporate or bureaucratic worlds only to discover that what we are running from replays itself in the yoga community too. As Jon Kabat Zinn said, "Wherever you go, there you are."

The gap between knowing about these ideals and actually implementing them is a complex and muddy place. Michael used to teach that these guidelines could be worked with through three different lenses. The first, the literal level, is easy to comprehend, although perhaps not easy to stick to. At this level "don't harm" means don't harm. But as soon as you start trying to implement a phrase like that, you run into bogs and forks in the road where the literal application can fall apart. Not eating meat is an example of non-harm in action; but what if you need meat to be healthy? What if vegetables are not available to you in winter? On this more metaphorical or compassionate level, your non-harm path may mean that you only cut down the amount of meat you eat, or only eat meat that is ethically raised and butchered. And then, if you delve deeper, you hit the realization that it's impossible not to do harm. Michael called this the koan level—the level where thinking or logic can't really help you. By the mere fact of our births, we're using up resources and harming the planet. Thousands of microscopic critters are dying, because we inhale them. We have to eat. We have to excrete waste, thereby producing sewage. We have to work. We have to put gas in our cars if we want to leave our suburban homes. So the assignment of non-harming is impossible: but we can still act in numerous ways to mitigate or cut back the things we do that harm ourselves, others, or the planet as a whole.

Tackling the yamas and niyamas takes mindfulness, curiosity, and work. But they are immensely helpful guideposts when we're struggling with conflict or decision-making. We're all striving to be a little happier, a little more at ease, and to make a meaningful contribution to the world. Yoga philosophy has a lot to say about caring for ourselves AND loving the world. In the end, they turn out to be the same thing.

Practice & Reflect

Journal:

- Think about an issue you've been struggling with in your life. You can choose something personal, or something political, or both—but narrow it down to one thing.

- Write it down and try to keep your description short: one or two sentences.

- We'll work with this further as we look more closely at the yamas.

First, Do No Harm: Ahimsa

If you don't stick to your values when they're being tested, they're not values, they're hobbies.
— Jon Stewart

The yamas, or ethical precepts, are where the rubber of our intentions meets the road of our everyday life. Keeping them in our awareness gives us a useful frame of reference for decision-making. They are not rules, but merely ways of thinking about our relationships to everyone and everything else we encounter. They are not black and white, nor should they be used to snuff out desires. We need our desires to keep us motivated and interested in the world. But desires need to be navigated, and sometimes restrained for the benefit of all.

Life decisions require energy and attention, and we never make them in a vacuum. When we're stuck in a dilemma, or a quandary (twice as bad), the yamas provide tools so we can exercise better judgment. They don't guarantee things will turn out the way we want them to, but at least we'll be able to rationalize why we made the choices we did. For impulsive people (i.e., me), they can also slow down the gap between stimulus and response, useful in and of itself.

Ahimsa is often described as the first principle of yoga and translates into English as "not-harming." We apply this to ourselves and others, and also we recognize that there's no actual separation between ourselves and others. Of course, we live in a world where we need boundaries, responsibility, and individuality. We need to be independent and look after ourselves to our best capacity, but we also need to understand how the choices we make ripple out. If I routinely trash my body with drugs and alcohol, that has an effect on my family, my friends, my employer, the health-care system, and the taxpayer. I may think I'm only hurting myself, but it's impossible to only hurt yourself.

Harm comes from our tendency to think that the world revolves around "I, me, and mine." We can't help this to some extent, because we're wired this way, but we also have the gift of our capacity for abstract thinking, insight, and imagination. We can read fiction, and imagine ourselves from another person's point of view. We can learn, change, and broaden our perspective and our capacity for compassion. We remain malleable until the end of our lives, if we choose to exercise our engagement with the world.

When we're working with ethical precepts like ahimsa, we can consider the three layers of insight—literal, compassionate, and koan—and also the three fields of activity—thought, word, and deed. I know. It's complicated.

Meditation practice can help us see with a little more clarity the thoughts that come up. We get to be continually annoyed by repetitive hits on our playlist of resentments, failures, regrets, and self-doubts. As we become more aware of our mental landscape, we can begin the difficult task of wrestling with harmful mental habits. Working with our more unflattering thoughts is difficult, because our instinct is to disavow, block them out, or become angry or disappointed with ourselves. But the point of this exercise is not to be good. The point is to stop perpetuating the pain. We can only work with the thoughts we're willing to welcome in. We have to start with kindness.

Recently I saw a wonderful animated short called *Animal Behaviour*.[6] The film featured a group therapy session with members that included a leech who was too clingy, a pig with an eating disorder, an obsessive-compulsive cat, and a bear with anger-management issues. Besides finding the film funny, I also realized that I have versions of all of these characters inside my own head. The psychologist who was leading the group in the film was a dog, and he had a dog's capacity for being non-judgmental, patient, and forgiving. I thought perhaps the voice I need to connect with is my inner dog. (I'm reminded of the joke about the agnostic dyslexic who lay awake at night wondering if there is a dog.) Perhaps God's love and a dog's love are analogous. Nobody loves you with as much soulfulness and purity as your dog loves you. Perhaps when you're beating yourself up, you can try to imagine what your dog might say about your foibles and work toward that level of self-compassion.

Words are a second level where we can cultivate non-harming, and a level where I'm aware I frequently fail. In our world of social media and instant communication, the power of words to translate into harm has been demonstrated in shocking ways. The arguments about political correctness versus free speech versus hate speech have never been more pertinent. Words are tools that we need in order to have relationships—they can bind us together or tear us apart. Words matter.

The Buddha taught some rules for communication. He advised us to ask four questions before speaking:

Is what I'm about to say true?
Is it kind?
Is it helpful?
Is this the appropriate time and place?
Can the person I'm speaking to hear it right now?

To make the best use of this advice, we need to slow down. In our hyper-speed world of Twitter and email, I wish we had a "Right Speech" app. My life would certainly be better for it.

Finally, we come to deeds. Most of us, with the possible exception of certain criminals, don't set out to hurt anyone. But we do harm all the time—to ourselves, to people we love, to strangers, to the environment. We might try to rationalize it away, but the deeper, more knowing awareness within is not so easily fooled.

Thing is, we can't entirely avoid doing harm, but we can work to cut back. We can also perfect the art of the apology. We can make efforts at reconciliation, and always keep in mind the abiding principle that not harming starts with ourselves. Nobody is advocating becoming a pushover or a doormat. Sometimes being willing to leave a relationship, cut someone out of our lives, or fight for a worthy cause are examples of non-harming. It's confusing, and it can be difficult. That's why ahimsa belongs in the virya section.

Practice & Reflect

Journal:

- Go back to the issue or struggle that you identified earlier.
- Can you write down a couple of ways that ahimsa might apply to it? Have you been harmed, or have you harmed someone else, or both?
- Was the harm in the form of thoughts, words, or deeds?
- How could you use right speech to address the situation?

Aparigraha and Generosity

Be content with what you have, rejoice in the way things are. When you realize there is nothing lacking, the whole world belongs to you.
— Lao Tzu

Aparigraha is often translated into English as not being greedy. The root *graha* comes into English as *grasp*, and the word *aparigraha* also means "not clinging," or "not being rigid." We can be grasping when we are trying to control what other people think or say about us. We grasp when we refuse to listen to other people's viewpoints, or when asked to go beyond our comfortable routines. We grasp when we try to maintain an "image" or a "brand." We grasp when we refuse help from others because that would alter our perception of who we are. We grasp when we attempt to turn back the clock and return to a world that doesn't exist anymore. I think of all the precepts, that this is the one I struggle with the most. At the root of it all is fear.

We live in a culture that admires and thrives on greed. We're all about consuming both material goods and experiences. In our consumer way of thinking, greed is the great motivator behind our whole economy. We all have healthy desires for basic needs to be met, including food, shelter, love, and companionship. We desire meaningful work, good health, and hobbies that bring us joy. But when do we ever have enough?

It's in our nature never to be satisfied. Once all of our basic needs are met, we just dream up new needs. Our logic seems to dictate that there's no harm in that. The economy is chugging along, and everybody's happy, except when we consider the disparity between the haves and the have-nots that has grown larger in the last few decades. The other issue with our multiplying and unlimited needs is that we're killing the planet. Seven billion people who all want to have the latest tech devices, convenient disposables, this year's styles, and wine-fridges for their kitchens are exceeding the resources the earth can offer. We've already wiped out 60 percent of the world's wildlife since 1970.[7] Are we really willing to trade birds, dolphins, or deer for more kitchen gadgets we don't use or that ninth pair of shoes?

And it's not just in the financial sphere that we take more than we need. We can be greedy for attention. We can be greedy for status, degrees, trainings, travel, or "likes" on Instagram. We can eat more than we need, buy more than we need, or even exercise more than we need.

The issue is not what we're going after, but why. In the Buddhist worldview, the explanation for greed is that it is the result of our sense of lack. Our real desire is to try to hold on to things that can't be held on to. We want to feel real and solid and safe in a world where the only constant is change and uncertainty. We'd like to be so successful that we'll be remembered forever, so that after we die some part of us will still be here. It's built into us to want permanence, but in the dimensions of the universe we know about, we're not so important. As the song goes, "All we are is dust in the wind." Our grasping is just the attempt to fill that hole in our psyche with distractions. That might feel depressing, but it can also be liberating. We can stop trying to roll that psychological boulder up the hill, and sit down and relax for a change. We might even have time to appreciate how beautiful the planet is.

So imagine I have a good job and money in the bank, but I'm still striving because I want more money to feel safe. I need to save for a rainy day, and for future holidays, and a new car and more things my nieces need; and when a street-beggar asks me if I can spare a dollar, I think, "No! I don't have enough." But in reality, I have more than enough. And I have thousands of times what he has. I can fall back to the idea that I'm more deserving than he is, but in reality in most cases it's just about circumstances. He got a mental illness, I didn't. I had supportive, loving parents, he didn't.

The opposite of greed is generosity and the cultivation of santosha (contentedness). We can aspire to be generous with money, or with time, or with attention. We could share more, and not with the intent of getting something in return. We could do things that don't lead to a pay-off or an immediate result. We can take care of the environment so that future generations can thrive with clean water, clean air, and food that is safe to eat. Yes, that might mean we have to make do with less. But buying less can also translate into more leisure time—time to enjoy the things that we do have. Cutting back and simplifying can have tremendous benefits for our health, and sometimes generosity can include letting go of the need to keep up with the Jones's. There is freedom in letting go of ideals and just being real. Instead of grasping for that "best self" in some imagined future, we could make the best of the selves we have now.

That's not to say that we shouldn't enjoy our lives or take holidays or eat ice cream. Nor am I saying that we should let go of our dreams and ambitions. Only that we stop and think about where there is more room for generosity and spaciousness in our lives, and that includes being more generous and kind to ourselves.

Practice & Reflect

Journal:

- Revisit the same issue you identified earlier.
- This time see if there is a place within it where the principle of generosity could apply.
- Could you let go of being "right" if that were necessary to resolve the conflict? Have you listened with generosity?
- Do you need to be more generous with yourself?
- Set timer for ten minutes.
- Write about how this yama might apply to your situation.

Honesty — It's Complicated

The ideal subject for totalitarian rule is not the convinced Nazi or the convinced Communist, but people for whom the distinction between fact and fiction (i.e., the reality of experience) and the distinction between true and false (i.e., the standards of thought) no longer exist.
— Hannah Arendt

To embody the principle of satya means to tell the truth, to be honest. It's a principle that seems out of fashion these days, where lying by powerful individuals goes unopposed and blatant misinformation is being spread far and wide by trolls on the internet. Perhaps we've needed to go through this developmental stage as a democracy to remember why truth is so important. Lies, unfortunately, have power.

On a literal level, honesty is easy to understand, but in practice, in relationships, it can be surprisingly complex. We all know that too much honesty, or poorly timed honesty can be harmful or injurious—like when your mother asks you if her new dress makes her look fat. Sometimes we have to choose not-harming (ahimsa) over being truthful. Sometimes we can be dishonest with ourselves (e.g., I really *need* $85 yoga pants). Sometimes honesty requires dealing with a painful issue that we'd rather avoid, or requires that we make an unpopular decision or deliver unhappy news. We may not always be rewarded for honesty, at least not in the arena of success and status.

Although it is true that paradoxes exist, and two opposing things can both be true at the same time, like string theory, satya is not about determining what is true. That function can be left to the scientists, scholars, investigators, and journalists. Satya means to be honest and tell the truth as you understand it. In this day and age, I would add, it also means to be open to new evidence—to be willing to take in new information, weigh it appropriately, and change your mind if you've been misguided or misled. To act from a place of honesty requires flexibility and humility.

By the same token, being honest requires some backbone and strength. Like the tale of *The Emperor's New Clothes*, honesty can require sticking your neck out. As the Buddha advised, you should be "a light unto yourself." When something is true, it can be tested and tried. You needn't take anyone's word for anything.

Some of the best tellers of truth are actually writers of fiction. Fiction as a form takes us on a journey into the life experiences and perspectives of other people. Going on this imaginary excursion can help us understand our fellow beings, because we tend to see our similarities rather than our differences. Fiction allows us to try on different consciousnesses, which also reflects the places where we've become stuck in our habits, whether personal or cultural.

Honesty is tied to yoga and mindfulness by the embodied experience of moment to moment observation, without the constant narration that slots every experience into what we already know. When we can prod our mind out of its usual rut, new insights come. I remember once ruminating about another person, and then realizing quite suddenly that what I was doing was projecting my feelings and thoughts onto them—that everything I was thinking was actually just "more me."

Whenever we have a new insight, or discover a truth, if we're paying attention, we can feel it in the body. Yoga teacher Richard Freeman explains it this way:

> When we practice the yoga of observation and we pay close attention to something, there is a residue of clarity and relief that is discernable in the breath and is actually felt in the body. It is similar to the sensations you might experience when you have been struggling to understand something and then finally "get it," or the feeling you get when you have been deceiving yourself about something and then at last admit to the truth; it is a feeling of relief, openness, cleanliness and joy.[8]

Truth-telling can be difficult, and it's not often rewarded. But honesty is still worth pursuing. If we can embody honesty in everyday interactions, life becomes much simpler. We don't get caught in a web of lies, perpetuate relationships that aren't beneficial, or find ourselves in compromising situations. We don't have to spend precious energy pretending to be something we aren't, or pretending to love somebody we don't, or avoiding people we've harmed. The short-term consequences can be a little uncomfortable, but honesty can help us heal. It can help us to move on. Honesty requires bravery, but like most skills, becoming more attuned to it can result in positive changes.

Practice & Reflect

Come back to the situation you've been journaling about, and now look at it through the lens of honesty.

- Have you been dishonest with yourself or someone else?
- Have you had expectations of others that don't match their expectations or capabilities?
- Have you avoided telling the truth because of uncomfortable consequences?
- Have you been close-minded or unwilling to entertain viewpoints that disagree with yours?
- Which is more important in this situation—honesty or not harming?

Not Stealing Is Harder Than You'd Think

Do what you can, with what you have, where you are.
— Theodore Roosevelt

The principle of asteya means "not stealing." At first glance this feels like an easy one. Few of us go out with the intent to steal things. And yet we do, all the time.

For one, we confine our ideas about stealing to commercial transactions like shoplifting, but in yoga and Buddhist traditions, the idea of stealing is broadened and includes an "energetic" perspective. Michael used to define asteya as "not taking what is not offered freely."

We can steal time from other people by constantly being late, or we can steal by monopolizing conversations and demanding that we be the center of attention. When we download movies illegally, plagiarize ideas, or hide our true income from the tax man, we're stealing.

Taking what is not offered freely can apply to relationships as well as things. Sometimes we're stealing when we ask for favors, because we know our friend is too kind to say no. We impose on them the role of the "bad guy," or boundary-setter. Once in a while these situations are inevitable (and it's not wrong to ask for help if you need it), but when it happens continuously it can be an energetic theft. And we've all been in relationships with energy vampires—people who take a lot of care and maintenance and who give nothing in return.

Asteya also applies when it comes to borrowing things. The difference between being offered something and assuming we can borrow it is a subtle one. The belief that someone won't mind is a form of projection and crosses a boundary, even if, in the end, it turns out that permission is granted.

In light of climate change and our consumption-oriented lifestyle, it can be said that we are stealing from future generations, stealing from all the other species, and ultimately from our own capacity for survival.

When we become slaves to ideas about what we should have and who we should be, we steal from our own enjoyment of life. When we dedicate too much energy to the treadmill, the stock market, or the cosmetic surgeon, we're stealing time from all the other people and activities we love. Fitness is important, financial responsibilities and self-care are important, but so are our relationships, time outside, spirituality, creativity, and fun.

The positive way of looking at this precept is to think about its mirror side: generosity, kindness, and contentment. Can we enjoy a more simple life? Can we spend a little more time discerning the difference between wants and needs? And can we be more giving of our attention, our energy, and our resources?

Like all of the other yamas, not-stealing is a function of not-harming ourselves or others. The work that this precept demands is to investigate and attend to the feelings of wanting, envy, or resentment that underpin our rationalizations for taking from others. When we recognize and acknowledge these feelings, we can work on resolving them, and on building our capacity to be generous—which is the antidote to stealing.

Practice & Reflect

Go back to the situation you've been journaling about.

- Does the principal of not taking what is not freely given apply to it?
- If yes, write a few bullet points about how.
- If no, jot down one or two areas or relationships in your life where you could be more generous.
- Write a plan for one act of generosity. For example, once a month I'll go help my grandmother with her household chores.
- Notice any resistance or emotions that come up.

The Wise Tending of Sexual Energy

*Ideas of where to go, how to be,
what to do, all these control trips
start to drop away. Already knowing,
there is no need for guidance. As
the poet Mary Oliver says, "Just let
the soft animal of your body love
what it loves." Giving the cow its head,
home is everywhere you turn.*[9]
— Edward Brown, "The Vision Cow Heads for Home"

A few years ago I attended an open house at a yoga studio where a woman was selling herbal wraps that promised to "get your sexy back." It sounded like "sexy" was a pet that could wander off, or a state of being that disappears if you make the mistake of aging or gaining weight. But the same promise was evident in everything about the studio: the skimpy outfits; the artistic photographs of stunning young women doing challenging postures, or remarkably-muscled men with copious hair doing one-handed balances on cliffs; along with the displays of vitamins and nutritional supplements that promised a return to youth and beauty. We all have a deep longing to be desired and cherished, sexually and emotionally. That the yoga industry takes advantage of this comes as no surprise.

The final yama is called *Brahmacharya*. Brahma was the Hindu god of creation, and *Brahmacharya* means "the wise use of sexual or creative energy." The urge toward intimacy and sexuality is innate and embodied within all of us. The ways we choose to express this drive are diverse and powerful. But sexuality is also influenced by a lot of ideas about what is right, how we should look, and how we should behave, that come from outside of our embodied experience. Our sexual feelings are affected by many external forces including culture, religion, politics, and economics.

Historically, it's important to understand that the early "raja" yogis and Buddhists removed themselves from their regular lives and livelihoods in order to practice, and studying yoga or dharma required celibacy. But the co-existing Indian epics and texts were abundantly sexual, and the Kama Sutra (250CE) is probably the earliest "how to" guide to erotic enjoyment. Later styles and versions of yoga did not always embrace the practice of celibacy in the same way, and sometimes described yoga as the reunification of the divine feminine (Shakti) with the divine masculine (Shiva)—a metaphor also for the coming together of body and mind. When we talk about sexuality and yoga, it's necessary to include the context of time, place, and lineage—because the teachings and traditions vary widely.

Brahmacharya requires reinterpretation if it is to be meaningful to modern practitioners, and many teachers and thinkers have done their best to do so. But it's never as clear cut as we'd like it to be.

Unless we were raised by wolves, and perhaps even then, we come "pre-loaded" with beliefs about sexuality. Many of those narratives run so deep, we have no inkling of their origin. One example is the long relationship between sex and shame in Western culture. It appears, based on historical artifacts and texts, that the Greeks were quite open and unrepressed when it came to sexuality and homosexuality. But that changed with the advent of Christianity and the teachings of St. Augustine.

For Augustine, the embodied and unpredictable aspects of our sex drive became conflated with sin and our humanity-wide fall from God's grace. Although he recognized the necessity of procreation, he believed we shouldn't enjoy it. Much of his disgust had to do with his inability to control the whims of his body with his mind. Augustine believed that our loss of control over our passions was directly related to original sin, and the blame rested entirely with Eve. Sin originated because man (the spirit) failed to exercise control over woman (the flesh).[10] Through the middle ages, as Christianity became dominant, sexuality became associated with lust, lust with loss of control, and loss of control with shame.

The philosopher-historian Michel Foucault was particularly interested in the origins of our sexual attitudes, proclivities, and drives. He argued that the only way to comprehend our "world of speech and desires" was to recognize that they are affected by a multiplicity of events that interact and influence each other. He said, "We believe that feelings are immutable, but every sentiment, particularly the noblest and most disinterested, has a history."[11] This history is not linear. While St. Augustine was tormenting himself about having erections, somewhere else in the world there were, no doubt, lots of people having blissful and shameless sex.

Foucault pointed out that many beliefs we take to be fact are actually created by discourse—in other words, the sum of what we collectively read, write, film, post, and more. Read any woman's magazine, and you'll be offered all kinds of "expert" advice about what is sexually "normal." But this advice is often based on beliefs and assumptions rather than truths, among them that there is a "normal" that applies to all people at all times. These days many articles focus on using medications, hormones, or other interventions to counteract age-related changes in drives or sexual frequencies. We've invented a whole new arena in which we can be "not enough." As discourse creates new expectations, those chatty "woman to woman" voices are often just marketers in disguise.

We can also fall victim to power structures like corporations or research foundations or governments. Foucault identified three main methods that may function as tools to objectify sexuality:

- "Modes of enquiry," such as Medicine or Biology or Psychology, which objectify individuals by making them case studies. In the late 1950s, Masters and Johnson famously conducted a large research study on matters of sex and sexual frequency, which became standards upon which individuals are measured (without regard to the accuracy of the self-reportage that they received or the conditions that supported the findings).

- The dividing of people into categories: sick versus healthy, normal versus abnormal. (Or as in the comedy *Seinfeld*, sponge-worthy or not.)

- Ways in which we objectify ourselves: selfies, photographs, buying magazines, joining weight-loss programs, working out so that our bodies become a certain "type."[12]

In any case, what we think we understand about our sexuality is only the tip of the iceberg. We are influenced by many power structures, beliefs, and commercial interests. A former professor of mine, Marie-Christine Leps, wrote, "Power functions not only through repression, but also through production and encouragement, by stimulating pleasures and ambitions, identities and habits."[13] So much of what we feel comes from within us (low self-esteem, desire or lack of it, fulfillment or lack of it) is being introduced subtly and surreptitiously from outside.

Of course, this relates back to the importance of inter-being and inter-dependence. And also to an understanding of the self as in flux and always changing—an art project rather than a concrete reality. A more mindful understanding of sexuality urges us to go back to our real embodied experience without all the window dressings, complications, and control trips.

Sexual acts come with potential consequences: emotions, expectations, sometimes infections, and sometimes children. Michael used to say that whenever two people become intimate, a third thing is created, even in gender-diverse relationships. But there is also danger in repressing sexuality, in avoiding intimacy out of fear, self-judgment, or a desire for control. Clearly we have to balance our natural desires for love and sex with moral responsibility, material concerns (e.g., can I support a child?), and our desires to fulfill other drives in our lives.

As modern-day practitioners struggle to understand and define what boundaries should be placed around sexual expression, it's clear that more needs to be done. In recent years a number of yoga and Buddhist teachers have been found guilty of sexually abusing their students. Current thinking in the yoga community emphasizes the importance of safety, informed consent, and the recognition of power imbalances. Yoga communities have acknowledged that clear, openly available guidelines and policies are necessary to manage and prevent potential problems. These can range from instructor dress codes, to policies about touching and hands-on assists, to guidelines about teacher–student relationships, and processes for making complaints.

Ideally, the path of yoga should help us to get to know "the soft animal of the body"—to be alert to its needs and desires, while maintaining care and respect for our partners. Letting the other influences drop away, we should have no need to spend countless dollars trying to buy our "sexy" back, because we'll understand that sexuality is a living, changing, and evolving part of our life experience. Like the "vision cow," if we ease up on ourselves, our bodies will know what to do. As we grapple with Brahmacharya, we learn to differentiate between wisdom, restraint, and repression. We gain an appreciation of our own sexual needs and proclivities against the background of what we're told we should want and need. Our relationships and our social structures could really benefit from a more open and deeper consideration of this creative, embodied energy that is wandering through us and between us.

Practice & Reflect

A useful way to work with wisdom and Brahmacharya is to view sexuality through the lens of the other yamas. Have a look at the summary of the yamas below and see whether the examples listed help to clarify certain difficult sexual situations (either hypothetical or personal).

Ahimsa (not-harming)

How can sex harm? Having non-consensual sex, using another person only for sex, having sex with a minor, being greedy, being selfish, objectifying other beings for our own sexual gratification.

Asteya (taking something that is not freely given)

Using photographs or social media to exploit, pressure, or get off on someone without their consent. Pressuring someone into sex, absence of consent, having an affair with someone who is not free. Or using power differentials to obtain sex. Or being dishonest to get sex.

Aparigraha (grasping, or taking more than you need)

Being greedy, addicted, rapacious. Never being satisfied. Needing to be amused, titillated, entertained. Abusing someone emotionally to get what you want sexually (e.g., "If you don't do it, I'll be forced to look elsewhere"). Or the opposite. Refusing to acknowledge a partner's sexual needs.

Satya (dishonesty)

Pretending to love someone in order to get sex. Avoiding issues in a relationship by having sex, or not having sex. Refusing to acknowledge desire and sexual feelings.

Churning the Ocean: How to Navigate Difficult Emotions

It is no measure of health to be well-adjusted
to a profoundly sick society.
— Jiddu Krishnamurti

Over the last few years, I've struggled with the feeling that the world has gone absolutely mad. It's been hard to digest what is happening in the news, and harder to work with the resulting emotions. I find it takes work (and support) not to descend into despair and anger.

The rate of change in the world, particularly in the last fifty years, has been exponential. New technologies have disrupted traditional ways of doing things, and we've made huge progress in areas like health care, communications, space travel, and physics. We aspired to make the world better, and in many ways we have, but in the process many people whose jobs have been eliminated by "progress" have been left behind. There are also those whose dissatisfaction with change has caused them to misdirect their rage at women, immigrants, environmentalists, people who are well-educated, Muslims, and others. The internet has allowed vast amounts of disinformation to be spread far and wide, and that misinformation has been used to foment distrust and hatred. In our lusting after progress, we've managed to unleash a hornet's nest of angry, frightened people who seem determined to cause suffering to all they define as "other." We've also managed to create an environmental disaster: the oceans are full of plastic, climate change is wreaking havoc, and we're responsible for a mass extinction of non-human species.

There is an ancient tale in the Vedas that provides a surprisingly appropriate lens through which to view the state we're in.

In Hindu mythology, the azuras (gods) and devas (demons) were often locked in a battle for supremacy, but now and then they would cooperate in hopes of attaining some boon or greater power (the way countries will cooperate at Olympic Games even when they're not getting along). Both groups were in search of the nectar of immortality (or compassion, depending on who you ask) and were told by a higher power that they could find this nectar (amrit) by churning the ocean—just like making butter. They placed the holy mountain, Meru (a metaphor for the human body), on the back of a huge tortoise and used a divine snake as a churning rope. The gods took hold of one end of the snake and the demons took the other, and they began to churn. As they built up momentum, and the ocean became a wild and frightening whirlpool, a terrible stench arose from the center of the mountain, and poisonous gases filled the air. The end of the world was imminent, so they called upon Shiva, who symbolizes pure awareness, to come and save them. Shiva flew down and sucked up all the poison, but he didn't swallow it (desire), and he didn't spit it back out (aversion). He held it in his throat with equanimity. The poison, *halahala*, is meant to symbolize delusion, or *avidya*, which means "a refusal to see things the way they are."

Sometimes when we go deep into a practice of yoga or meditation, we start to churn up old emotions or traumas that we've repressed or never acknowledged. Some students will leave a practice at this point, because if there isn't enough support, their unearthed vulnerability can feel toxic.

The metaphor also holds true when it comes to political movements: in the seeking of change, all kinds of poisonous and unacknowledged stuff comes up. We have to deal with this personally and socially. Adding fuel to the fire doesn't help, but neither does curling up in a ball and pretending everything is fine. What I'm trying to work on is awareness, compassion, patience, and readiness to step in if and when I see opportunities to promote reason and kindness. Sitting in this place is really difficult, and I have to practice starting over a lot.

The key to it all is awareness. But awareness takes work, cultivation, and discipline. We start small, in our own bodies and minds, and gradually expand outward. The more we are aware of what is happening within our homes, communities, countries, and the world, the more it comes back to holding space between feeling and acting. Figuring out how to respond to issues requires research, discussion, compromise, and time. Nothing can be resolved by Twitter, and knee-jerk reactions usually create nothing but chaos.

Everyone has their own methods of coping, and I've discovered that some lucky people don't worry about the world at all. But I'm trying to worry about one day at a time, and to breathe, and to enjoy the warmth of the sun, and chocolate, and reruns of *The Vicar of Dibley*. My hope is that if a crisis that I can actually do something about arises, I'll respond appropriately, not with anger but with compassion.

Practice & Reflect

Journal:

- Make a list of the things that you find helpful for calming and soothing yourself. Aim for at least five. No need for them to be deep or meaningful, just useful to you.

A Tool for Working with Self-Judgment

Because true belonging only happens when we present our authentic, imperfect selves to the world, our sense of belonging can never be greater than our level of self-acceptance.
— Brené Brown

During the 2020 pandemic, I've had the luxury of ample time to go for long walks along the rural roads close to my home. And though I found the fresh air and proximity to nature nourishing, I noticed a startling amount of discarded trash in the fields and ditches. And with each passing day, I noticed it more, and found it increasingly irritating. Then I started making excuses not to walk. I'll just work in the garden instead, I thought, because I'd rather do that than be confronted by the mess made by littering pigs with no appreciation for wildlife or their neighbors.

Does that sound peaceful or yogic?

There are moments when I feel like a hypocrite, because I still have such negative and judgmental thoughts. Not all the time, but not infrequently.

Sometimes as we grow in our capacity to slow down, get still, and really look at our hearts and minds, we can stumble into a hornet's nest of ugly emotions. And just like trying to get into Pigeon Pose for the first time, we might be blindsided by just how much of a pain in the ass these feelings are. It's upsetting when my image of who I think I am, or who I want to be, slams into the wall of the actual things that go through my mind. Or worse, when conflict with other people or unexpected situations make me doubt my own integrity. I often feel ashamed, disappointed in myself, or otherwise unworthy of the title of "yoga teacher."

This conflict between who I want to be and how I actually feel is a type of cognitive dissonance. I often find myself caught between two potential worlds: the comfortable habit-world and the aspirational freedom-world. The voyage from one to the other requires a lot of inner work. When I find myself in a difficult emotional place, it is always accompanied by a deep vein of self-criticism. And then I can double-up by judging myself for having so much self-judgment.

A number of psychotherapists and Buddhist teachers I know teach a useful technique for working with these deeply ingrained feelings. Vipassana teacher Michele McDonald was the first to develop this mindfulness-based technique, known by its acronym RAIN.

The first step in this process is to *recognize* (R) the stories and emotions that are coming up. We can't ever get clear on what we're feeling if we're constantly busy and on the move. Stopping or slowing down gives us the space we need to be more aware of the self-talk that's going on in our minds, as well as the discomfort that may accompany it.

The next stage is to *allow* (A) the feelings we're having to become fully conscious. Often this requires honesty and humility. We have to let go of the idea that we have to be good or feel good all the time. Relaxing our resistance to feelings we don't like means that we can make space for them, and once we can, they don't cause as much distress. We simply acknowledge them and perhaps do a little self-soothing with a simple gesture (like putting a hand on our heart) or a mantra like "It's just a feeling, it will pass."

Once we've determined the full extent of our real feelings (as opposed to just the ones we like), the next stage is to explore and *investigate* (I) them. Part of investigation means unearthing the stories and experiences that underly the emotions. The process can look like a series of questions: Where am I feeling this in my body? What is the story I'm making up about this? What was the trigger that got me here?

Finally, the last stage requires *nurturing or not-identifying* (N): recognizing that having negative feelings doesn't make you a bad or negative person. You may require some help, or some support to get through whatever is causing your distress, but the feelings are arising out of conditions and causes, and as such, it's usually possible to transform them. And even if you're not successful, you can at least be compassionate toward your own suffering and recognize that being hard on yourself is neither necessary nor helpful.

So in the case of my outrage about the litter, the first stage is recognizing that I am truly emotional about this. My emotions include anger, fear (for the environment and a sustainable future), and a deep, sad desire for the world to be different than it is. The second step is actually allowing myself to fully feel those emotions, which is difficult.

Investigating the feelings requires looking at the storylines behind them. One of them is that there are "these people" who are driven by complete selfishness, disdain for the environment, and hatred of people like me who are trying to defend it. And although that story really *feels* true, I have no evidence to support that. I have many friends who tease me about being a "tree-hugger," but none of them would throw their takeout garbage out the car window. Much of the garbage is just the result of wind blowing people's recycling out of their bins, and the fact that some of the people living here are disabled or otherwise unable to pick up the trash once it blows away. And my story about how people should behave with respect to nature is mainly the result of my own upbringing and love of the outdoors. Some people are just so consumed with basic survival that they've no time to even notice it. That doesn't mean they are "pigs" but rather that they have different priorities from me. I will never like the fact that they toss garbage from their vehicles, but it doesn't make me superior to them.

When it comes to the nurturing or non-identifying stage, I'm still figuring that out. For one thing, it's important to recognize that just because this issue makes me angry doesn't mean I'm an angry person. I have a lot of grief about the loss of the natural world to work with, but also I can focus more on effective ways to change the situation. I decided one day to start picking up the garbage. I was overwhelmed quickly by the enormity of that task, but I think if I can recruit some helpers, I could make it a fun event and do something more productive than feeling bad about it. I hope that eventually, I'll be able to walk again without feeling irritated by the mess. Or I may just have to reframe the way that I live with the irritation—like an oyster making a pearl. As they say, into every life a little RAIN must fall—it's another useful tool to hold onto, as we keep putting one foot in front of the other.

Practice & Reflect

Journal:

Think about a situation or relationship that causes you pain. Write your answers to the following:

- Recognize/Stop: When and how will I make time to do this work? (Be specific.) How do I describe the problem I'm having?

- Allow: What feelings come up? (Use words, images, or even sounds.)

- Investigate: What stories go with this feeling? What do I actually want? What remedies would make me happy?

- Nurture/Non-Identification: How can I care for myself better in this situation? What am I saying or believing about myself that is adding fuel to my suffering? Who can I go to for help or support? Can I revise the stories I'm telling about this problem?

Water Is Precious

Canada, the most affluent of countries, operates on a depletion economy which leaves destruction in its wake. Your people are driven by a terrible sense of deficiency. When the last tree is cut, the last fish is caught, and the last river is polluted; when to breathe the air is sickening, you will realize, too late, that wealth is not in bank accounts and that you can't eat money.
— Alanis Obomsawin

In May 2000, during an arduous backpacking trip near Parry Sound, I came down with what I thought was a case of the flu. There's nothing quite like having to relieve oneself every fifteen minutes on a group excursion in rattlesnake territory on the Canadian Shield. There were no bathrooms, and finding a private place without poison ivy and enough soil to dig a hole was an adventure in itself. When we got to our campsite, my friend Barb sent me to bed and went down to a lake to filter some fresh water for me, because I'd finished all the water I'd brought from home. By the time evening rolled around, I was feeling considerably better and chalked the whole episode up to dehydration.

Sunday evening when I got home, there was a message on my answering machine from a friend letting me know that the whole town was under a boil-water advisory. I lived in a third-floor walk-up in Walkerton. For the next month I carried bottled water up the thirty-six steps to my apartment, and put bleach in my dishwater. I was extremely fortunate to get off with a mild case of *E. coli*—six other people died. Although I spent a lot of time on the toilet during that surreal summer, we all received health-monitoring, compensation, and a provincial inquiry into what went wrong.

I learned from this experience just how much we take clean water for granted, and how important it is to our health and happiness. Shockingly, more than a hundred First Nations communities in Canada do not have clean drinking water, and have not had it for years—yet little has been done about it. All over the planet, humans have blithely and knowingly polluted the water we depend on for our survival, with no plan or budget to clean it up. Contaminants like lead are becoming commonplace, and aquifers are drying up. As the climate changes, scientists predict clean water will become increasingly scarce.

One of the central tenets of Yoga and Buddhism is the principle of interdependence. All forms of life, from bacteria to elephants to humans, directly impact one another. If I dump toxic chemicals into the lake, eventually the effects of that will show up in my body, or the body of someone I love. If I'm pouring chemicals onto my lawn, I shouldn't be surprised when the frogs start to disappear (the return of the spring peepers every March is one of my greatest joys). In the yogic view of the world, humans have great power, but they don't exist separately from the rest of the natural web. Historically, millions of us have been taken out by bacteria, organisms too small for us to even see. We're kidding ourselves if we think we are somehow above the laws of nature. When we damage the environment, we damage ourselves. In a culture that espouses "me first" or "jobs first," we destroy the crucial resources that are fundamental to our survival. As a bumper sticker says, "There are no jobs on a dead planet."

Balancing survival with caring for the environment is a work in progress, and I am not holding myself up as a role model. I also struggle to be content, live simply, and to stand up for nature in whatever situations I can. I try to find battles that are big enough to matter and small enough to win. Regardless, I like to remind myself of the *Star Trek* phrase, that human beings are just "great big bags of mostly water," and that the hydrological cycle means we're all sharing the same resource. So when the environment is under attack, for me at least, it's personal.

Practice & Reflect

Journal:

- Choose a cause that you care about. Write it down. Identify one or two organizations that are currently working for that cause, and decide whether and how you would be willing or able to contribute.

Appropriate Anger

Anger is the deepest form of compassion, for another, for the world, for the self, for a life, for the body, for a family and for all our ideals, all vulnerable and all, possibly about to be hurt.
— David Whyte

Women aren't supposed to feel anger. And if we dare admit to it, we express it at our peril. When men feel small, afraid, and powerless, anger is not only expected but encouraged. But for most of the women of my acquaintance, anger is not permissible or socially acceptable. We're supposed to be more rational (there's a paradox), more positive, and more interested in making sure no feathers are ruffled or feelings hurt. When horrific injustices happen in the world, we're encouraged as women to turn away, to focus on our families, our waistlines, or our health; on nurturing and peacemaking both at home and at large.

But calling for peace from our place of safety and privilege does nothing to examine or change the structural violence that caused these unjust events in the first place. It does nothing to help the income inequality, racism, lack of opportunity, and institutionalized unfairness that helped instigate these problems. Our reluctance to engage with anger denies the importance of what the anger signals; it gets in the way of resolution and insight.

Anger can be toxic, and it can certainly be dangerous and detrimental, but it's also a deeply embedded early warning system. In the face of injustice, we *should* be angry. When the factory up the road is dumping toxic waste into the river, and we recognize the threat to survival that this entails, anger is the rational response. When we witness bullying, disrespect, or any of the myriad forms of threat or violence in the world, anger is appropriate. There is an energy in anger that drives us to get up off our butts and do something. We don't have to act rudely or negatively, but we need to attend to the danger. Anger should be explored and managed, not repressed.

Because we tend to be dualistic thinkers, we often label anger as "unbecoming," especially for women, and fail to recognize its usefulness. It's true that uncontrolled anger is a poor character trait, but it's an effective instigator. Warriors know better than to be driven by anger because once unleashed, it's not easy to control. Nor is it a pure emotion—when explored thoughtfully, it comprises a spectrum of other emotions such as fear, frustration, shame, projection, and helplessness. Anger needs to be attended to and looked after, acknowledged and legitimized. Otherwise, it leaks out and involves itself in places and relationships where it has no business. For example, the daughter who is angry about her inability to cope with her mother's dementia may misdirect her anger at the nurses and personal support workers who care for her. Repressed and unattended anger becomes a contagion.

The whole point of interdependence, the jewel of yoga practice, is that every choice we make has vast and often unforeseeable consequences. Whether for better or for worse, the ripple effects of our judgments will eventually encompass us all. When a frightened or confused person makes a poor decision, it triggers others to make poor decisions, and more and more innocents die. I don't have any answers, but I do believe that to change the causes of violence, we have to be willing to change ourselves. We have to feel and acknowledge where we are violent, where we are greedy, and where we are afraid. We have to be willing to feel our anger, to take care of it and process it, allowing it to be there without identifying with it, without believing that it defines us. That's a lot harder than turning off the news, or listening to soothing music on Spotify. But this is the work of a bodhisattva, an awakened being.

Acknowledging and working with anger is hard on the ego. A few years ago, just after the Paris attacks[14] in 2015, I was sitting in a coffee shop in Toronto when a man from the Middle East put his backpack down at the table next to me and asked if I could keep an eye on it while he went to the bathroom. I said yes, but the whole time he was gone, I stared at that pack and wrestled with the fear of "What if?" I saw my own paranoia, my own racism, my own delusions and projections about an ordinary, harmless guy.

Yoga is about controlling the runaway horse that is our mind on fear. You can't tame the horse until you confront whatever is spooking it, and those factors tend to be what you repress, ignore, or pretend don't impact you.

What we do matters, and we can make positive changes, but first we have to accept the fact that we're not supposed to feel peaceful and happy all of the time. Being oblivious to the suffering of others might help you avoid feeling bad, but it's also a way to squander your life and take for granted all the gifts you've been given. Anger is important; it's a good motivator, as long as it's recognized, acknowledged, and acted upon in productive rather than harmful ways.

Practice & Reflect

Journal:

- What is your relationship to anger?
- Was anger something that was expressed or repressed in your upbringing?
- What does anger feel like in your body?
- How do you know when you're becoming angry?
- How do you usually behave when you're angry?

Goldilocks Yoga

The middle path is the way to wisdom.
— Rumi

If you've ever been to a fitness class, you've heard the phrase "Listen to your body," or the variation "Honor your body." My students and I joke that if we listened to our bodies, we'd be at home on the couch with a glass of vino and a bag of Cheetos. As a teacher what I'm conveying when I use that phrase is that I want my students to recognize the difference between the mild discomfort of stretching (or of making a muscular effort) and the pain of a potential injury. For athletes this is a no-brainer, because they have a keenly developed awareness of which signals to pay attention to. But this is not true for most of us, particularly as our bodies experience changes such as injuries, arthritis, or even aging. Often we don't know we've overdone it until a day or two later. We're like a modern-day Goldilockses looking for a pose that's "just right."

As a teacher I'm dancing between asking too little and asking too much. At one end is the desire to challenge students, to press them to go beyond their fears and ideas about their limitations. This is sometimes called *sthira* (effort). At the other end of the spectrum is my desire to do no harm, to keep everyone safe, relaxed, and injury-free (*sukha*). I struggle to find a middle ground, and this is complicated by the fact that every person has their own "right effort" set-point. Some people routinely push themselves to the point of exhaustion or injury and should in fact learn to do less. Others *need* pushing. I make an effort to balance these extremes myself, and recognize it's impossible for me to determine what is right for someone else. All I can do is get to know my students really well and do my best to reflect them back to themselves.

Communicating about what you're feeling is important, and yoga classes aren't always conducive to this, because we like to focus on breathing and sensation. Too much chatter in a class can be distracting and annoying, so we also have to find a balance between speaking up and just doing our own thing. Every teacher has their own way of handling this.

Another dilemma teachers face is giving too much information about where or what you should be feeling. If I say, "This movement should stretch your hamstrings," I may be overruling your experience—derived from the unique conditions of your body. But if I don't give you any information, you might be feeling sensations, such as back pain, that signal there is something wrong with the way your body is aligned or that your body isn't ready to do this particular pose. It's a tug-of-war between providing the freedom to explore versus the ensuring safety of containment.

Honoring your body, for me, means that you recognize you are the only one who can really know what you're experiencing, and you have the right and the obligation to refuse to do anything that doesn't feel useful or helpful to you. Yoga is the process of trying to figure out the perfect balance between too much and too little, between effort and ease. And this relates to everything we do in our lives—we're always struggling to find the middle way.

Practice & Reflect

Journal:

- What is your tendency when it comes to effort and ease?
- Do you tend to push yourself too hard? Or do you feel like you need pushing?
- Is this different in different areas of your life?
- Do you do better when you have someone else you're accountable to?

Embodying the Warrior

I learned that courage was not the absence of fear, but the triumph over it. The brave man is not he who does not feel afraid, but he who conquers that fear.
— Nelson Mandela

Recently in a city close to where I live, a Muslim man leaving a family picnic was beaten nearly to death in front of his wife and two young children by a couple of racist goons. In years gone by, the response to this would have been prolonged shock and outrage. But this time, the reaction barely extended beyond the twenty-four-hour news cycle.

The past five years have revealed an undercurrent of ugliness, greed, and delusion in our society that I find shocking. A small minority of deeply disturbed people have been supported, emboldened, and set into action by some extremely powerful, and frankly, evil people (evil in the most banal, pathetic, and narcissistic of senses). Their genius has been in mobilizing groups of people to attack one another while they quietly plunder resources, balloon their already massive bank accounts, and dissolve all the regulations that might have held them in check. They perpetuate lies and attack the media, the academics, and the scientists. Historically, the intelligentsia were always among the first to be shipped off to the gulag or the prison camp. I know I will be accused of being alarmist, but frankly, it's time to be alarmed.

More and more often, isolated and delusional people perpetrate violent attacks on innocents. They create fear, leading to mistrust and more isolation, and the whole cycle feeds back on itself. Hoping this phenomenon will resolve itself will not get to the bottom of it.

The primary ethical directive of yoga is ahimsa, which means to do no harm. But contrary to popular opinion, this does not equate to inaction. The other day I stumbled on a quote paraphrased from the Reverend Dr. Martin Luther King: "Our lives begin to end the day we become silent about things that matter."[15] And for those on the receiving end of hatred and violence, he said, "In the end we will remember not the words of our enemies but the silence of our friends."[16] Sitting back, turning off the news, and just hoping that this is going to go away is not an adequate response. Hope is dangerous when it's not accompanied by action. Hoping, for instance, that new technology will reverse climate change, without being willing to make any changes or alterations in our own lifestyles, is the reason we've had decades of inaction.

In yoga we practice a number of poses named after Virya, the great warrior. These poses embody strength, being grounded in reality and the ability to stay with what is difficult. The warrior stances require flexibility, balance, and sustained attention.

The Tibetan Buddhist tradition has its own forms of warrior, including female deities known as *dakinis*. These are fierce, frightening entities whose name translates roughly as "sky-dancers." They embody the energy of anger, but are free from aggression or hatred. They represent the transformation of anger into skillful action. They take the useful, motivational energy and use it to champion truth, destroy delusions, and create the space for better solutions or outcomes to arise. They are a force of fierce love—like the ferocity of a mother bear when her cubs are threatened—a reaction that is not driven by ego, or based on being right, but rather born from a need to protect life.

The aim of the yoga warrior is to transform anger rather than renounce it: to acknowledge it, take care of it, and use the energy beneath it to defend truth, life, and the interconnected web of all beings. We battle against the forces of hatred, delusion, and narcissism. We practice the Warrior Poses, and we practice mindfulness—not to transcend the world, but to live in it more wisely. We need to act, in whatever small ways we can, mindful of our own afflictions (greed, fear, ignorance)—and we can't wait until we think we've achieved enlightenment to do it. Sitting on the sidelines hoping that the pendulum will swing back toward truth and reason on its own is unwise. We only need to look at history for abundant proof of the horrors we're capable of. What's needed in such dark times is cultivation of courage, and an expression of love that is not driven by egotism.

The principle of virya inspires us to be brave, support one another, and choose at least one small battle. Our actions can be as simple as writing letters, donating to a good cause, supporting journalists, volunteering, or even just calling someone on their racism or homophobia. The culture of yoga would be much improved if we focused less on bikinis and more on dakinis. As individuals we can drive positive change, but we have to hold our ground, get over our need to be liked by everybody (big personal stumbling block for me), and be willing to fail with grace.

The warrior has a code of ethics that she stands on, and she's willing to take risks. When you're practicing your Standing Warrior Poses, think of them as a practice for holding ground and resisting ignorance, shame, and blame. Practice being uncomfortable and challenged, and then take it off the mat and out into the world.

Practice & Reflect

Journal:

- What obstacles do you encounter when it comes to standing up for yourself, or for someone else you care about?
- What are you most afraid of?
- What do you feel in your body when you imagine being in a conflict?

Part Five: Joy

Find a place inside where there's joy, and the joy will burn out the pain.
— Joseph Campbell

The next step on this journey, after we've become more mindful, curious, and disciplined, is to explore the territory of joy. A lot of ink, both real and virtual, has been dedicated to teasing out the difference between happiness and joy. For our purposes I can only state what I mean when I talk about joy, and leave the arguments to the philosophers and psychologists.

Happiness, to me, is a state of contentment and pleasure. Often it's contingent on some external condition being met, such as, "When I find secure employment, I'll be happy." Joy has more intensity than happiness. Joy is often more transient, more invigorating, and more effervescent. Joy is more likely to make you forget your daily concerns, however briefly.

Joy is not something that we create, but rather something we receive—spontaneous, sparkling moments of grace that often disappear as unexpectedly as they arrive. Going to someone's cottage for a weekend makes me happy, witnessing a meteor shower on the way there brings me joy. Joy can bring us to tears.

Unlike happiness, joy can be present in the midst of calamity. Roberto Benigni's film *Life Is Beautiful* is an illustration of the power of joy. The protagonist's father, Guido, is a man whose astonishing imagination and capacity for mischief create moments of joy for his son during their internment in a concentration camp. The film was indeed beautiful, but I wept so much I had to watch it in two sittings. It left me feeling wrung out, and yet full of wonder—in spite of the horrors and cruelty it also depicted.

Joy can arise even while one is in a black mood. I remember once during my marriage break-up, when I felt like a walking storm-cloud, I caught myself singing along to a tune on the radio by Great Big Sea. In that brief, revelatory moment, I knew I was going to be okay.

The key to joy is not to seek it, but rather to clear a path for it to come through. The tasks of the steps we've already covered can help this happen. Being attentive and less judgmental, too, can help. When we escape our habitual grooves and our unceasing self-talk, we make more space for what's joyful. And best of all, for the most part, it's free. When we invite joy into our lives, we can pass it on to others through our own creativity, whether expressed in the kitchen, the studio, or driving to work. Joy begets joy.

Practice & Reflect

Journal:

Practicing gratitude is a great way to open ourselves up to more joy.

- Make a list of five things you are grateful for, and/or five things that bring you joy.
- If you're really committed, you can make this a daily practice.

A Bright Light in a Dark Time

*Do not be dismayed by the brokenness of the world.
All things break. And all things can be mended. Not
with time, as they say, but with intention. So go. Love
intentionally, extravagantly, unconditionally. The
broken world waits in darkness for the light that is you.*
— L.R. Knost

I've always been deeply curious about the world, have felt it's important to watch the news and pay attention to politics. I did my master's thesis on happiness and utopianism, and I was drawn to my mentor by his commitment to activism. When you believe in interdependence, you believe that what happens to people on the far side of the earth will have its impact here in time. Everyone is connected. But sometimes watching the news breaks my heart. Sometimes I feel like we don't deserve the space we inhabit on this planet. I think I took up yoga and meditation precisely because of this despair, and because of my practice, most of the time I have the tools to cope with it.

Still, some events are just overwhelming: terrorist attacks, school shootings, the vitriol online, the diatribes against women (what century is this?), and the bizarre state of the United States. At times I have to grope around in the darkness for something firm to hold on to. And recently, during one of those dark moments, what occurred to me was a memory of a man I met whose name was Bright.

Years ago I was traveling alone in Asia, during my marriage breakup, when I came down with dengue fever and gastroenteritis. I wound up in a youth hostel in Jakarta, flat on my back for more than two weeks, so sick and so sad that I honestly didn't care whether I lived or died. And there was this gorgeous young man from Nigeria who adopted me like a stray cat. He brought me food every day and insisted that I eat it. He went shopping for me and found me ginger ale, which required him to take a bus downtown. He kept me company, and together we watched *Baywatch* and *The Price Is Right* in the hostel lobby. Every time someone won a prize, he was so full of joy you'd have thought he'd won it himself. He even tried to find me Jell-O (I had dreams of Jell-O), although he'd never seen it and thought it sounded disgusting. He was a student waiting for a visa to join his brother in Malaysia. He'd fled Nigeria because his family had been politically active, and a few loved ones and friends had been "disappeared" or killed. He did all of his caregiving purely out of generosity. He wouldn't take a penny from me, nor did he want any favors. The day he arranged for me to get back to the airport, the day he carried me to a waiting cab, I gave him all my contact information—and then I never heard from him again.

Sometimes when events around the world leave me shaking my head, or when things feel dark and dreary, I think back to Bright, and how he reached out to me, a privileged, white, Canadian woman who took for granted more freedom and wealth than he'd ever had. At a time when I felt completely broken, he was a model of kindness and love. He showed up, did good things with no moralizing or preaching, and then disappeared like a shooting star, before I'd even realized he'd changed the trajectory of my life. I think a world that has Bright in it is worth saving, and I hope that someday I can be someone else's Bright.

Practice & Reflect

Journal:

- Make a list of two or more people who have changed your life in a positive way.
- If you're so inclined, and you can still connect with them, send them a note to let them know.

Awe and Samadhi

*The rest of this must be said in silence
because of the enormous difference between light
and words that try to say light.*
— Rumi

The final stage on the yogic path is called samadhi. Perhaps it's not accurate to call it a stage, because for most practitioners it's a brief and fleeting experience that functions something like a psycho-spiritual orgasm—it's all-encompassing and makes you want to go back for more. You can't really stay in samadhi and function in the world, but the promise of this joyful mind and body state is tantalizing.

I should add here that the discussion of samadhi is esoteric and somewhat problematic. *The Yoga Sutras of Patanjali* describe layers of samadhi that I don't have the expertise or experience to comment on. I've had some delightful meditations, but the problem with calling these samadhi is that language fails to capture these states, and there's no way to verify that what I felt is, in fact, samadhi. By definition, these altered states are beyond language. Some people call them bliss states; others refer to them as enlightenment experiences. At present, none of us really know what they are, only that they are associated with practice and have a long history.

Any time we try to talk about complex mind-body experiences, we run the risk of projection. Some teachers describe samadhi as a state of integration, intimacy with all life, or union with the Divine. Whatever you choose to believe, it's likely that if you practice yoga and meditation consistently and remain with it for the long haul, you'll have some fascinating experiences. These may come in the form of sensations, visions, or sounds. They will appear spontaneously and then disappear, and you may spend many months or years desperately trying to get back to wherever it was that you went. Conversely, if you've never had a samadhi experience, it does not mean that you're doing something wrong. None of us can really say what causes them, and they aren't a given.

In my experience, the closest analogue to samadhi would be the sensation of awe. We feel awe when we witness a beautiful sunset, come across a stunning vista, or encounter a dolphin while swimming. We can also be awed by art, music, or incredible feats of athletic ability, like those performed by Cirque du Soleil. What marks an experience of awe is the sense of being completely absorbed—our inner narrator goes silent, and there's no sense of "me" doing something. We become one with whatever we're experiencing.

Researchers who study awe describe it as a powerful emotion that can either bring us together or be used as a tool to manipulate us. Beau Lotto, a professor of neuroscience, discovered that people who've experienced awe come away feeling more willing to take risks, more comfortable with uncertainty, and willing to redefine their perceptions of who they are.[1] Lotto reflects that these qualities are essential for creativity, optimism, and positive social behaviors like tolerance, empathy, and trust. The experience of awe, or, I would argue, samadhi, can help build bridges and improve relationships. But awe can also be used to intimidate or threaten. Witnessing the power of a stealth fighter jet at an airshow can be awe-inspiring, but if you live in a war zone or grew up during military conflict, you may feel fear rather than delight. Great displays of military equipment are often used to enhance the power of the dictators who wield them, and to ensure that people are aware of the harm authorities can inflict if they so choose.

Samadhi experiences are generally mind-opening and joyful, but they should be understood with respect and caution. Because these moments are so powerfully motivating, it's possible to get caught up in efforts to reproduce them that are unhelpful or destructive. I've known a few yoga students who've abandoned their spouses, families, and jobs on a quest for bliss that's ended up being disastrous for both themselves and their loved ones. And many a cult leader has taken advantage of these "peak" experiences to convert believers. If you've had bliss moments in your practice, it's helpful to have a teacher or community to discuss them with, and to keep in mind that the point of yoga and meditation is to manage better in your daily life, not to run away from it.

Practice & Reflect

Journal:

- Have you ever experienced a moment of awe or bliss?
- What were you doing at the time?
- What did you feel in your body?
- Did you try to replicate it? If so, what happened?

Compassion Makes Us Happier

I have just three things to teach: simplicity, patience, compassion.
These three are your greatest treasures.
— Lao Tzu

The field of positive psychology has become immensely popular. It's the study of what is right with people as opposed to what is wrong with them, with the aim of discovering how we can all be happier.

Multiple research studies have reaffirmed what most people know intuitively: practicing compassion increases happiness and self-esteem and benefits us on a physiological level. It increases levels of the "love hormone," oxytocin.

Like all prescriptions for good health (diet, exercise, etc.), knowing this does not necessarily help us. Most of us are so overwhelmed with the demands of our daily lives, we can't imagine how we could possibly fit in compassionate acts. Or at the opposite end of the spectrum, if we have trouble saying no, we can experience compassion fatigue (giving too much of our time and energy to the point where we become exhausted).

Part of our dilemma can be a result of misunderstanding what compassion is. It can be helpful to return to the etymology, the root meaning, of the word. *Com* means "to be with" (as in community), and passion means "suffering" (as in the Passion of Christ). To act with compassion does not mean that we need to go out into the world and fix everything. In fact, the expectation that you can "fix" people is pretty much the opposite of compassion. Often the most compassionate acts are little things, like shoveling a sidewalk, or taking a little time out to call someone who is lonely. It can be as simple as being attentive and patient when listening to a friend.

When we think about practicing compassion, we have to negotiate a balance between healthy boundaries (making sure our own needs are looked after) and doing things without expectation of reward. Sometimes we need to receive help rather than give it, and by asking for help, we allow others to receive the benefits of giving it.

In yoga we practice compassion keeping in mind the principle of non-harming (toward both self and others) and the premise that we need to develop loving-kindness toward ourselves first (maitri). If we cannot be inwardly loving and kind, it's impossible to extend this energy to others. When we do helpful things for others, we reap the benefits of our actions through our own sense of purpose and fulfillment. And sometimes, though it's not our objective, "What goes around, comes around."

All of this sounds lofty and idealistic, but the truth is, it's a practice. We do it little by little, we repeatedly fall on our butts, we keep starting over, and we will never graduate.

Practice & Reflect

Loving-kindness (Metta) meditation:

- Set timer for fifteen minutes.
- Find a comfortable meditation posture.
- For the first two minutes just relax and settle in.
- Then for the next three minutes repeat the following mantra:
- *May I be happy. May I be healthy. May I be safe and free from danger. May I know wisdom and compassion.*
- Then, imagine someone you love and care about, and for the next three minutes repeat to yourself:
- May _____ be happy. May _____ be healthy. May _____ be safe and free from danger. May _____ know wisdom and compassion.
- Next, choose someone that you feel neutral about. Repeat the same mantra for the next three minutes, but dedicate it to this person.

- Finally, for the last few minutes, choose someone you've had a hard time with or whom you actively dislike. Repeat the same process for the final few minutes.

- If you find this too difficult to manage all at once, you can space it out. For the first few times, just send the loving-kindness to your self and your loved ones, and then, eventually, branch out to others.

"Wild Thing, You Make My Heart Sing"

Nature is not a place to visit. It is home.
— Gary Snyder

Among the things that bring me joy—including friends, family, art, music, comedy, chocolate and such—the natural world is among the dearest. I have always loved birds. As an enterprising seven-year-old, I wrote and illustrated a book about the birds that visited our yard. Alas, it went unpublished. Not long afterwards I received the gift of rubber molds that I could fill with plaster to create cardinals, finches, and blue jays. I still can close my eyes and remember the smell of plaster, the strange warmth of it when it was setting, and the breath-holding as I turned out the molds. I painted and shellacked dozens of birds, and presented them as gifts to forbearing uncles and aunts.

Birds still thrill me. We keep a feeder and suet in our backyard and witness a wide variety of regular visitors. In my view, no artist can create anything that equals the beauty of a wild bird: the colors, the intricacies of feather, beaks, and claws, the remarkable fragility and lightness of a bird in the hand (I've rescued and revived quite a few over the years, and buried just as many). The sighting of a rare bird, like an indigo bunting, has me running around with a camera and over to tell my neighbor, who is as enchanted as I am.

The study of birds, ornithology, has advanced by leaps and bounds since I was a child. As a devotee of science, I've learned from shows like *The Nature of Things* and *National Geographic* that my suspicions about crows were true: they're remarkably intelligent. They communicate with each other in two languages; one for family and another for the larger community. Their family caregiving can be multigenerational, with aunts and uncles hanging around to help care for new babies, and they will mourn a fallen brother or sister, gathering to sit silently in a crow funeral. Not only can they recognize human faces, but they can teach their children to avoid specific humans.

The more time that we dedicate to studying and observing the natural world, the more we recognize how completely ignorant we humans have been. I believe that something deep within us still feels our connection to the wild. Research on the mental health benefits of being out in nature supports this. But somehow we haven't translated this knowledge into meaningful action. Developers and businesspeople are still keen to pave over everything to build sprawling subdivisions, because "People need homes." But people need nature too. No big box store has ever come close to bringing me joy, but the sight of a deer with fawns in my backyard will have me over the moon.

I'm not keen to live through the winter in a hut without heat or hydro, but I'd certainly be willing to sacrifice many "mod-cons" if it meant ecological health could be restored. To me, nature is sacred, the land is sacred, and all of it depends on a balance between how much we take and how much we do *for* the environment. We're only just beginning to understand the complexities of the natural world, like the vast networks of microscopic fungi that partner with trees to keep them healthy. We've forgotten the essential truth that we are mammals: we depend on the soil to be healthy, the air to be clean, and the water to be free of contaminants and pollutants.

I take joy wherever I can find it, which most often for me is in the wild: in the flora and the fauna; in the fish, the feathered, the furred. There are people in the world who espouse the view that nature is there to be conquered, or that its only value lies in resources that can be extracted and sold. But those who have divorced themselves from the natural world are living in denial, believing that humans are separate and "above" rather than dependent and intertwined with the ecosystems that support us. This strange (at least to Indigenous peoples) belief in our separateness is likely to wipe us out eventually. The natural world is indifferent to us, but we need it—*I* need it—to be well.

Practice & Reflect

Get thy butt outside:

- Schedule at least an hour sometime this week to go for a walk or a bike ride somewhere natural: a forest, a park, or a garden. Walk in silence, or go with a friend.
- Make a note of the plants, birds, and animals that you see. Take pictures, if you're so inclined.
- Pay attention to whatever forms of life (or death) you encounter.

Grace After Meals

In ancient times cats were worshipped as gods;
they have not forgotten this.
— Terry Pratchett

Recently I attended a talk by experimental filmmakers Emily Vey Duke and Cooper Battersby.[2] I find their films and photographs provocative, challenging, darkly humorous, and sad. They said they are "committed to being in therapy forever." I find their openness disarming and doubt that any amount of therapy will normalize them, but the whole charade is endearing. They would like to be better people. Their therapists would like them to be better adjusted. Though, there is no heroism in adjusting to a culture that is, in itself, seriously flawed.

But what interested me most was their relationship with cats.

Cats figure largely in their art and their life. We had a discussion about the dangers of anthropomorphizing[3] animals and our tendency to project our feelings onto our pets. They reminded us that the animals we know and love have no ability to dispute the ideas and emotions we're projecting onto them. In other words, it's a one-way street. This all sounded logical at the time.

But today I am at home with my own cat, Thomas, who is making a case for cat consciousness and cat person-hood that is oblivious to all my lofty ideas about projection and fancy words like *anthropomorphization*. My cat, at the moment, is celebrating the arrival of his lunch. We have these rituals, you see. About an hour before lunchtime, he begins a series of activities—practices that start with earnest supplication (winding around my ankles, visits to my lap, toothy kisses to the tip of my nose) and then escalate to mischief (usually involving some keyboarding, the theft of pens, the relocation of papers, the knocking over of small ornaments, and then the stealing and indecent misuse of my toothbrush). My part in this ritual is to resist all of his efforts until he discovers a behavior that I can no longer ignore, and then I get up and dish out the Friskies.

But the ritual is not over. After gobbling up his lunch, Thomas completes what I call the victory lap. He produces a complicated vocal medley of happy meows and runs around the whole house, skittering across the laminate, sometimes losing his footing on the corners and hip-checking the walls. I cannot think of a single, logical explanation for this behavior other than that it's an expression of joy. In my heart I know that Thomas is, in many ways, a superior being, and our relationship is much richer and more complicated than scientists and psychologists give us credit for. Thomas looks up to me a) because he's short and b) because I facilitate the opening of the can, and I look up to Thomas because he is an acute student of my behavior, he is warm and sensual and pretty to look at, and he is moved to joy by a small dish of foul-smelling turkey and cheese. If only humans could be so easy to love.

Practice & Reflect

Call to mind an animal that brings you joy, whether currently or in your past.

- What characteristics of that animal bring you the most satisfaction?

Journal:
- Make a list of the qualities you appreciate.
- How do you (or did you) express your affection toward that animal?

The Wisdom of No Advice: Memories of an Afternoon in Bed

Being heard is so close to being loved that for the average person they are almost indistinguishable.
— David W. Augsburger

Years ago when I was working in home care, I met a lovely woman I'll call Betty. She was in her late sixties and having a terrible time with balance. I saw her a few times one summer but couldn't solve any of her problems. She was going off to see a specialist to try to get to the bottom of it. About six months later, I was asked to go and see her again, because they'd discovered the source of the problem, and unfortunately, it was a brain tumor.

I let myself in to her home, as was our arrangement, and found her curled up in bed. As I entered the room with my briefcase and clipboard, she gazed up at me and said, "Put that stuff down and crawl in."

I was taken aback. I'd never had that particular request before, and all the trainings I'd had about professionalism, boundaries, goals, reports, and accountability were dancing around in my head.

She saw my hesitation and said, "I'm not going to say a word to you unless you put down all of that crap and get in here." And with that, she patted the space beside her and folded her arms in a gesture of determination.

So into the bed I got: without my professional armor, without forms, paperwork, or questionnaires, and at a loss as to what I was doing. And then we talked.

She told me about her youth, her years as a dancer, her marriage, her divorce, her struggles, and her triumphs. Her ex-husband had recently fallen on hard times and was living in her renovated garage. He'd installed an intercom so that she could call him whenever she needed anything. She talked about what really mattered to her now that she was into her final weeks. She showed me a sweet muslin bunny that one of her friends had brought her. It was scented with lavender, and she thought it was the most joyful thing ever. She also told me that she intended to eat Kentucky Fried Chicken as often as she wanted to, since she no longer had to worry about her cholesterol.

The things I had been sent there to help her with, like getting into the shower, were of no concern to her. What she wanted to tell me that day was to take off the mask and just be present, be a human chatting with another human, without trying to fix or change or control anything.

We talked for over an hour, and when I got up to leave, she gave me a hug and said goodbye. She said, conspiratorially, "Just tell me that I'm your favorite."

I did.

I drove home profoundly moved. When I sat down to write my report to the case manager, I had nothing to say other than "Client reports that her needs are met." The case manager, a wise veteran nurse, just smiled at me and said, "She's my favorite."

Betty died not long afterward.

I still think of her whenever I smell lavender, or whenever I watch the bedtime scene from *The Sound of Music* where Maria sings to the children about her favorite things to quell their fears about the storm outside. Betty taught me that day that it's the little things, the little joys that sustain us through the darkest of times, and that when all of our ideas and self-importance and agendas get stripped away, what's left is the best, most original part. She also taught me that being heard is far more important than I'd ever imagined. Betty gave me a great gift that day, and in many ways—without one word of advice—she pointed me toward the life that I have today.

Practice & Reflect

Journal:

- Think of an example of advice you've been given that is no longer useful or that has become an obstacle for you.
- Write about the circumstances and consequences of that advice.
- Who gave it to you? How old were you? How did it affect you?
- When did you start to see the problems the advice was causing?
- What obstacles and emotions come up in connection with that advice?
- What might it mean to let your baggage go?
- Who or what might assist you in that process?

Part Six: Relaxation

The graveyards are full of "indispensable" people.
— Unknown

When was the last time you felt completely relaxed? Some people seem to have a natural talent for relaxation. I am not one of those people—which as a yoga teacher is hard to admit.

At the end of every yoga class, we practice Savasana, or Corpse Pose. Partly, we do it as an opportunity to relax and feel the benefits of the physical work, but it's intended also to be a little nod to the Grim Reaper. Corpse Pose is meant to remind us that one day we won't get up from the mat, and the world will go on perfectly well without us. As much as we feel the weight of all our responsibilities and commitments, we needn't carry them at all times. The Corpse Pose signifies that we're not as indispensable as we think, and knowing this can lighten us.

Relaxation can be elusive; in our attempts to achieve it, we often miss it. For instance, we decide that to relax we'll book a week in the Caribbean to get away from it all. We book the trip, commit thousands of dollars, spend our evenings and weekends packing and preparing, log extra hours at work to get everything caught up before we go, arrange the dog-sitter, and then finally board our flight, absolutely exhausted. Once at our resort we eat too much, drink too much, sign up for too many excursions, and then get back on the plane and head home to our newly inflated debts. If we could learn to relax without having to run away from our lives, wouldn't that be simpler? I'm not against travel—I think it's awesome—but wouldn't it be more fun to travel without the complications of trying to decompress on a tight schedule? What if we could structure our lives with more simplicity and relaxation built-in, so we don't need to go away to unwind?

We all need a certain level of stress in our lives. Without any challenges or projects, we can feel sluggish, disconnected, and depressed. But the balance between not doing enough and doing too much is fraught with issues of self-identity, expectations, and habits. Some of us are so used to living on the edge of exhaustion that relaxing feels weird and unsettling. We sabotage it either deliberately or unconsciously by taking on more projects or more debt.

In this journey toward awakening, relaxation is a natural progression from the other skills we are learning. As we become more mindful, courageous, and clear about our values, we learn to trust ourselves and know that we "have our own backs." Gaining insight into the expectations that drive us, whether internal, external, or both, we are more selective about what we take on. Once we become enough for ourselves, we can let go of trying to be all things to all people, which comes as a tremendous relief. Then, ideally, we can relax anywhere, because there's nowhere that we need to get to. Wherever we are is good enough.

Practice & Reflect

Silence break:

- Plan for twenty minutes of silence somewhere in your day. You could go outside and walk, or stay inside with a cup of tea. But here's the catch: no sensory input beyond walking or drinking tea. No phone, no podcasts, no radio, no conversation, no TV, no reading. Twenty minutes of not taking in anything beyond your immediate surroundings.

- Do notice what comes in through your sense "doors": the sounds in the room or outdoors, the scents, the colors, the light or shadow, hard edges and soft edges, textures, weight, and so on.

Journal:

- When you're finished, list ten things you noticed.

The Ways We Run Away: Relaxing Versus Avoiding

Numb the dark and you numb the light.
— Brené Brown

One of my favorite Buddhist teachers, though I've never had the pleasure of meeting her in person, is the venerable Pema Chödrön. A well-known author, she is also the head teacher at Gampo Abbey in Nova Scotia. I always find her funny, relatable, and ever-so-wise. Her book *The Places That Scare You: A Guide to Fearlessness in Difficult Times* is one that I return to over and over. Within it she tackles many ways to broach our fears, including that we must get to know them well, rather than running away.

In the chapter "Tapping into the Spring," she provides a taxonomy: ways that we avoid going to the emotional places that scare us.[2] What I find fascinating but also troubling is that we often turn to these things looking for succor, comfort, and relaxation, and by doing so we inadvertently make things worse. We confuse avoidance with stress relief, and escapism for relaxation.

Chödrön's first category of avoidance activities are the distractions we use to soothe ourselves so we can ignore uncomfortable feelings. She calls them "the lord of form" because they are all external to our embodied experience and include a broad range of entertaining activities such as shopping, eating, exercising, drinking, or phone calls. None of these behaviors is good or bad; each is just a placeholder we use to put off dealing with problems or emotions we don't like.

A second type of escape valve is something Chödrön calls "the lord of speech." This category includes the beliefs and "isms" we use to give ourselves the illusion of control and certainty about the nature of reality. These include religion, politics, philosophies, and belief systems. Again, there's nothing inherently wrong with these except that they can become barriers to being in the moment, or being intimate with the person or situation with whom you are sharing the moment. When we default to our beliefs, we often close the door on any evidence that contradicts us and to people who disagree with us—resulting in intractable quarrels that lead nowhere.

Finally Chödrön describes a category she calls "the lord of mind," which includes our attempts to achieve special spiritual or mental states that allow us to avoid uneasiness or escape from our reality. Examples include drugs, alcohol, spiritual highs, adrenaline highs (e.g., skydiving, running), and falling in love. All of these experiences can be wonderful and exhilarating, but they can easily become traps, because they are so addictive. These pursuits may become ways to run away from relationships that need attention, or life changes that need to be made.

I openly admit to having tried everything on this list, and also, that I'm still pretty cozy with the three lords. The question that I have to ask myself, constantly, is whether I'm drawn to something for the sheer pleasure of it, or whether I'm using it as an avoidance technique. Am I having a glass of wine to delight in the taste, or to dull down an unhappy mood?

It feels odd to go toward what's uncomfortable versus away from it. The skill is to learn to relax in the midst of discomfort; to be curious rather than fighting or fleeing; to stop trying to fix things. Instead, we must try to feel the full range and spectrum of emotions crossing our interior landscapes. Certainly there are times when diversion and avoidance are legitimate and useful strategies for short-term survival—but in the long term, psychological work can pile up and overwhelm like unopened email newsletters.

It may be possible to avoid dealing with our emotions, relationships, or work stress for our entire lives, but doing so will ultimately diminish our capacity for ease. It can even make us sick. Getting to know our own "release valves" is a useful pursuit. I once made a list of my top five, because I adore the movie *High Fidelity*, about a man who continually runs away from vulnerability and commitment, and who loves to frame everything in his life in terms of top fives.

Being aware of your habits is always the first step toward change.

Practice & Reflect

Journal:

- Make a list of your top five "escape valves."
- How do you know, when you're enjoying your escapes, whether the enjoyment is pure or is driven by a desire to avoid a negative feeling?
- Who do you talk to when you're feeling difficult emotions? If you don't have a confidant or therapist, how do you deal with these emotions?

Losing One's Head

Exhaustion is the drug of choice for conscientious anxious people.
— The Stoic Emperor

One of the reasons I became a yoga teacher is that I am, at heart, an anxious person who ought to have a yoga teacher on speed-dial. My inability to sit still, which I believe was inherited, manifests itself in people-pleasing and constant overcommitment. Most of my life I've juggled multiple gigs while simultaneously volunteering, taking courses and planning social events. My modus operandi was to keep saying "yes" until I was too exhausted to continue or too overwhelmed to meet all the expectations I'd optimistically agreed to. When I felt like my head was going to explode I'd realize something had to give. At this point I'd resign from some responsibilities and deal with the fallout: a profound sense of failure. I'd relax long enough to lick my wounds and then sign up to do something else.

But then the gods sent me a sign.

I was gazing out the kitchen window one day, and noticed an odd-looking ball of grey fluff sitting on the edge of the bird feeder. I had a bad feeling about it and went out, armed with the shell of half an avocado (which I had been eating) and a paper towel. Sadly, the oddity turned out to be the head of a nuthatch. Just the head. I used the paper towel to pick it up, carried it over to the bush in the avocado shell coffin, and buried it. The question was how a perfectly beautiful little nuthatch came to lose her head so dramatically.

If there were an avian *CSI*, I might not have had to speculate. Possibly, it was the neighbor's cat, but I found it hard to imagine a scenario where the culprit leaping from the ground could come away with only the torso. The more likely suspect would've been a small hawk. I once witnessed a sparrow hawk taking out a chickadee on our deck. It dove so swiftly that I was unsure of what I'd seen until the hawk landed on the lawn to readjust its hold on the lifeless little body. The chickadee did not suffer; that I know.

So there I was, left only with my sense of wonder and the play of speculation. Nature is unkind, or at least unaffected by any sense of narrative. Nuthatches are born. Nuthatches are killed. Then it occurred to me that perhaps nuthatches also overcommit themselves to too many activities, and in a fleeting moment of inattention they explode at the bird feeders of people with similar character flaws.

But it was probably a hawk.

Practice & Reflect

Journal:

- Do you feel like you are doing enough? Or are you feeling overwhelmed?
- How do you decide which opportunities to take on and which to let go?
- What things have you committed to that you wish you hadn't?
- Can you make an escape plan to create more space and time for yourself?

The King, the Prince, and the Sands of Time

Once, a powerful king named Jasper lived on the shore of an azure sea. He woke in the mornings to the music of the surf, building and receding like a deep, relaxing breath. He loved nothing better than to rise before the sun and slip down to the jetty to fish. If the weather was particularly fine, after breakfast King Jasper would call for his servants to bring down some large, regal canopies, and he would conduct his business while keeping an eye to his fishing rod.

The king lived in a sprawling complex that housed his staff, his children, and their children too. His youngest grandchild, Ambrose, a pensive boy of eight years old, loved to come down and sit with him. Because he was quiet, and happy to play by himself, the king enjoyed his company. Ambrose passed his time building sandcastles, collecting shells, drawing on the beach with sticks, and doing all the other things eight-year-old princes like to do.

On one particularly beautiful day, the king was determined to get in some fishing, despite having to meet with his advisors. He arranged for chairs and refreshments to be brought down to accommodate them, and brought extra fishing rods so they could join him as they talked.

The first meeting was with the minister of agriculture. He was a stout and fidgety man, prone to overdressing, hence he perspired profusely in the heat. The minister exchanged pleasantries and sat down heavily in a cushioned rattan chair.

"I am happy to report, Your Highness, that our harvests have been abundant and our stores are full. We have more than enough food to feed our citizens and plenty to trade elsewhere. But," he said, "I am concerned that in our neighboring country of Umulu, the population is growing at a faster rate than ours, and their land isn't nearly as fertile."

"Go on," said the king, re-casting his line.

"My advice," said the minister, "is to build a great wall, to protect our lands should there be famine in Umulu."

"How long would that take?" asked the king.

"The expense would be great, and more taxes would be needed," the minister said, gravely. "But I expect the project could be completed in six or seven years."

"Thank you for your report," said the king. "I will let you know my decision."

The next appointment on the roster was the minister for economic development. He arrived on horseback wearing jodhpurs and fancy riding boots. He sat down in the chair offered to him and accepted a beer from a nearby servant.

"Our economy is doing well, Your Highness," he began. "But I want to report an opportunity that I think we must act quickly to take advantage of. In the Kingdom of Eiselan, many days from here, our prospectors report they've found a deep vein of gold. If we act quickly, we can purchase that land before the Eiselans become aware of its value. We will need to dispatch our best negotiators, and you must attend the meetings to ensure that our financial offer will be received in good faith."

The king nodded and took a deep swig of his beer. "How long do you expect these dealings to take?"

The economic advisor looked down at his feet. "Probably

a year, at minimum. But on a positive note, we can use some of the profits to build the wall that the agricultural minister is proposing."

"I suppose we could," the king replied. "Let me think about it, and we'll meet again in a fortnight."

The king stood up and looked around for Ambrose, who was playing with shells just a few feet below the dock. Satisfied that he was safe and well, he returned to his chair to prepare for his next meeting. The military advisor was next to arrive, flanked by two of his generals.

"What do you have to report?" said the king.

"Our borders are secure and we have no immediate threats. But our spies in Lesceste have reported that a new weapon is being developed. We don't yet know what it is, but I'm recommending that we act preemptively."

"Meaning…?"

"We should plan an attack," the minister said. "We will have the advantage of surprise, and we can mobilize our forces more quickly if we act before the rainy season comes."

The king sighed. "And how long do you think this project might take?"

Looking first to one general, and then the other, the advisor responded, "The initial assault will take six to nine months, but we expect our militia will need to occupy the territory for five to ten years. You will, of course, be required to lead the regiments into battle, as a display of our unity of purpose toward this cause."

The king promised to consider this proposition, and the military advisors marched away. When they had disappeared from view, the king stepped away from the pier and sat down on the sand next to his grandson.

Tousling the boy's hair with affection, he asked, "Did you hear any of the men talking today?"

The boy nodded, and continued arranging seashells into an elaborate mosaic.

"If I do as I've been advised," said the king, "I will be away in battle for months, at best, and then away in Eiselan for a year, and then supervising the building of a wall for another six or seven."

Ambrose looked up from his project. "That's a very long time to be away. I will be grown up by the time you come home." And then, looking suddenly wise beyond his years, he asked, "Grandpa, if you go do all of those things, and everything goes well, what will you do when you get back?"

The king looked out at the water, and then gestured at his fishing rod, which leaned against a post at the top of the jetty. He said, "I would sit down here with you every day and catch us some beautiful fish."

Ambrose stood up and dusted the sand from his shorts. He moved in front of his still-seated grandfather and placed his small hands on his shoulders. "You know," he said, "you can do that now."

And the king returned to his chair and cast his line back to the ocean.

Having Enough: Cultivating Contentment

Gratitude is what you feel when you want what you already have.
— James Clear

Have you ever kept a gratitude journal? For those who haven't heard of it or tried it, the practice consists of writing down three things a day that you're grateful for, so that you become more aware of what's good in your life. Taking a few minutes each day to think about gratitude is a way to actively work toward contentment, which is one of the niyamas in the path of yoga. Cultivating contentment, or santosha, is not something that gets a lot of press in our culture, except perhaps in the self-help sphere. But Marie Kondo's best-selling book on *The Life-Changing Magic of Tidying Up* is an example of one way to cultivate santosha, which is to simplify and declutter. Sometimes it's not necessarily a physical decluttering that we need, but rather a social or emotional one. Sometimes we've made too many commitments, or taken on too many projects. Sometimes santosha requires a pruning of our ambitions or the events in our social calendar.

To cultivate santosha is to cultivate contentment with what we have. We live in a society that makes it hard to achieve this. We're always being told that we need to do more, achieve more, lose ten pounds, and become something "better" than what we are. Santosha is about accepting and being grateful for what we have now. So if you don't have a *Yoga Journal* body, you practice appreciating the body you do have: the body that got you out the door this morning, the body that got you to class. We still want to work on challenging ourselves, but we create that challenge by going inside and feeling our way through the sensations, instead of comparing ourselves to external ideals. When we are confronted with a messy kitchen and a pile of dishes, we practice being grateful we have dishes, we have food to mess them up with, and we have hot running water on demand. The practice of santosha is about identifying what is right about our lives, what is right about our bodies, what is right about our relationships. It's about taking charge of our own inner peace, instead of letting others dictate what is needed.

Santosha should not be used as an ideological tool to deny the suffering of those who are struggling economically, socially, or mentally, nor should it be a rationalization for maintaining the unfair divide between the haves and have-nots. Rather, it's an internal dialogue that examines the question of how much we really need, and our unconscious ideas about what constitutes a good life.

In this time of environmental crisis, we've also got to examine the ways in which our greed is affecting the planet. Many yoga studios, churches, and ecological organizations have compiled lists of suggestions (santosha pledges) about how each of us could rein in our consumption and lifestyles for the good of our health and the sustainability of the planet. Examples of santosha pledges include actions as simple as adjusting the thermostat, using cloth bags for groceries, and stopping the use of non-essential pesticides and weed-killers. We all have opportunities to live more lightly on the earth, and it's just a matter of changing our habits.

Getting in touch with this contentment can allow us to be more peaceful, more generous, and more pleasant to spend time with. When we feel content, we have more space in our hearts and minds for others, and the time and space to relax.

Practice & Reflect

Journal:

- Make a list of five things you would be willing to do to live more simply and gently on the earth. For example: I will eat two vegetarian meals per week, or I will not purchase water in plastic bottles.
- If you are stuck for ideas, refer to an excellent online resource called "The Earth Peace Treaty Commitment Sheet." [3]

A Series of Successive Approximations

It is good to have an end to journey toward; but it is the journey that matters, in the end.
— Ursula K. Le Guin

There seem to be two breeds of people on earth: those who are clear from a young age what they want in life and how they are going to go after it, and those, like me, who have never felt a clear sense of purpose and are constantly struggling to come up with one.

Although I wrote a lot as a child and a teenager, I never really thought of myself as a writer. For one thing, I didn't generally write fiction, and I didn't know any writers. I came from a family of tradesmen, nurses, teachers, and janitors. I was the first person in my family to go to a university. Writing as a profession existed in a different universe. I was also shy, uncertain, and awkward. I developed an early habit of listening, spying, and surmising, because outright asking was bold and unbecoming behavior for a child in the era when we were instructed to "speak only when spoken to." I couldn't imagine being a journalist and having to ask people difficult questions for a living.

My yoga-teaching career and my writing have become paths only through what could be described as a series of successive approximations. I would set out in a direction, discover it was a mistake, make a correction, get a little bit closer, discover another error, change direction again, and so on. Through this process of stumbling and making course corrections, combined with the machinations of fate, I have finally found myself in a groove that makes me happy most of the time.

The strange thing is that I always worked hard to create clear goals and intentions for myself. I read all the self-help and career-advice books. I took surveys in magazines. But for all my planning and intending, I never seemed to end up where I thought I should. The more I tried to will myself toward a commitment, the worse things seemed to turn out.

Yet I cannot say I regret these misadventures. Once, I decided that maybe I should become a wilderness guide or outdoor education teacher. I enrolled in and finished the Wilderness Survival Program at Georgian College. This is what I learned: I hate to be cold and wet, the bugs love me more than anyone else, my severe phobia of caterpillars eliminates the better part of a month outdoors, most wild edibles taste really, really bad, and in a gruesome survival situation I would probably choose death. What I gained from this experience is Barb— one of the best friends I've ever had, a joy to spend time with to this day—and of course, some great stories.

We have so much pressure to "reach for the stars," "know what you want," and "to want more." There is nothing wrong with having aspirations and ambitions—they're healthy—but only when we don't cling to getting the results that we are expecting.

The more relaxed, albeit winding path is one where you just try things. You take a job, you learn where your talents fit (or don't fit), and gradually you move closer to the career that makes you feel useful and fulfilled. You follow your bliss, not by planning or taking personality inventories, but by trial and error. Often, you end up somewhere that you never expected to be, but that nonetheless makes you happy. Plans are helpful, so long as you are willing to change them. Clinging to plans, especially in our unpredictable and ever-changing world, can often come at the expense of growth and contentment. The pandemic we're living through now has created a unique opportunity for many of us to reflect on whether our choices to date have been conducive to our overall health and happiness. Softening up about planning and controlling means learning to trust yourself, and to trust your feelings and intuition, but without bypassing your brain.

Successive approximations can land you in a happy place. Yes, it is slower than the direct route, but it might also be more interesting. You don't have to be clear about where you're going, because there is no destination—just beginning after beginning after beginning. As the saying goes, if you love what you do, you'll never work a day in your life.

Practice & Reflect

Journal:

- If you were to try a new direction, either personally or professionally, what would it be?
- What could you do as a first step?

The Ugly Duckling

To study the self is to forget the self. To forget the self is to be actualized by myriad things...
— Dōgen

Regardless of what culture we grow up in, we learn much of our way of being in the world from the stories and tales that are handed down from generation to generation. Stories arise out of what Carl Jung described as a collective memory: a consciousness that is common to all of humanity. The same or similar stories appear in multiple areas of the world, even when there was no known contact between those geographical areas.

My favorite fairy tale is the story of "The Ugly Duckling," because I've always found it hopeful. The ugly duckling is a misfit. She doesn't look the same as her cohorts. She doesn't behave in the same way. She tries to fit in and fails. She feels alone and unwanted. I'm sure most people have felt this way at some time or another.

People often assume misfits are clueless, or don't care to fit in. Those things can be true. But the misfit is often acutely aware of her short-comings. I can, for example, give you an elaborate list of what separates a model from a non-model when it comes to physical traits. I can explain every feature of my own body that falls short. Not that any of it matters. As a kid in high school who couldn't afford to be "in style," I could always tell you exactly what was in style, which brands, and which colors. Fashion is, in my view, far more about conformity than about self-expression. You get to express yourself, but your choices are predetermined for you. Most people who are really imaginative and original in their clothing choices get labelled "outlandish," not fashionable.

The crux of "The Ugly Duckling" story is that her suffering boils down to a misperception. The duckling isn't actually ugly; she just doesn't see herself. She doesn't have the experience or vantage point to recognize that she is not isolated, nor is she "less than." The ugly duckling's problem is that she hasn't found her people. She's trying to be something she's not, because she doesn't know what she really is. Once she grows, she matures into a body that is more foreign and more beautiful than anything she can imagine. She discovers that she is a bird of a much larger and more powerful description. She's meant to be a swan.

In my life I've met so many swans who thought they were ducklings. So many men and women trying to conform to someone's idea of what they should look like, who they should love, or what careers would be meaningful. We go about hating our careers or hating our relationship situations without being willing or open-minded enough to do anything about them. As we grow, and if we're willing to keep learning and trying new things, chances are that we will stumble on the things that make us feel at home, and the activities and people who make us happy. The duckling doesn't fix her problem for herself. Friendships, failures, and time are what allow her to become what she was meant to become.

Sometimes, rather than constantly seeking our "true self," it's better to let go of our ideas of self-hood and just relax into the flow of our day-to-day lives. When we stop worrying about being enough or measuring up to an imagined standard, we can stop being so hard on ourselves. From that more relaxed place we can be more natural, flexible, and spontaneous. We're more likely to respond authentically and appropriately to challenges that arise. By forgetting about our identity, we become genuinely eccentric, because we're not living in our heads and over-analyzing every move we make. Letting go of our imagined self allows our repertoire of emotions, behaviors, and actions to expand. And being more eccentric and free is the most attractive trait imaginable—it has its own gravitational pull.

Some faith in our own basic goodness is required. Trusting ourselves is not something we can do in isolation. Our friends and families provide the mirroring we need to learn and grow into our true natures. And sometimes as we mature we need to leave relationships that are unhelpful, so we can find the ones that allow us to shine.

Whenever I see a swan, I think about that feeling—that graduation from conformity to liberation. Swans are big, beautiful, and unapologetic creatures. They never worry about being enough; they just swim, rest, and fly according to their own needs and rhythms. And that freedom from self-consciousness is attainable if we choose it. We can all open up to the "myriad things," which is another way of describing the "everyday everything."

Practice & Reflect

Journal:

- Is there a situation in your life where you feel you don't fit?
- What does that feel like in your body? What emotions come with that feeling?
- Is not-fitting a way of creating self-identity, i.e., are you creating that separation yourself, or does it feel like a product of other circumstances?
- With what person in your life do you feel like your most authentic self?

JUST BREATHE

Breathing in, I calm body and mind. Breathing out, I smile.
Dwelling in the present moment, I know this is the only moment.
— Thich Nhat Hanh

Yoga is uniquely suited to help us relax and calm down. The combination of movements and the stretching the physical postures (asanas) provide stimulate the release of feel-good chemicals in the body. The attention to sensation and moment-to-moment awareness helps us focus on what's actually happening in the present instead of ruminating about the past or worrying about the future. But by far the most powerful tool we have for calming down is the breathing practices collectively known as "pranayama."

I teach a wide variety of breathing techniques in my classes, because there is no better tool for joining body and mind. The respiratory system is the only system in the body that is innervated by both the somatic, voluntary system and also by the autonomic or "unconscious" nervous system. The respiratory system can act as a bridge (over troubled waters) precisely because it has these two types of wiring.

Rolf Sovik[4] describes the respiratory system as having three parts: voluntary, non-voluntary, and involuntary: The voluntary system allows us to hold our breath, play a wind instrument, sing, or whisper, or whoop. The involuntary system means that our breathing doesn't stop when we fall asleep at night, and it automatically knows to speed up when we need to exert physical effort. The non-voluntary system has to do with the way our thoughts and emotions affect how we breathe. When I get tense and worried about meeting a deadline, my breath gets short, tight, and shallow. The limbic part of my brain, where my emotions live, exerts an influence on the deep, old part of the brain that controls the regulation of breathing. Fortunately this non-voluntary response can be tempered by conscious acts of respiratory kindness. A deep inhale with a long, breathy sigh on the exhale can release the sensations of tightness in the tissues of the body, and lessen feelings of fear or frustration.

The term for the breath-training techniques is pranayama. In Sanskrit "pra" means moving, "na" means always, "yama" means to restrain, and the "a" in front of yama negates it. In short, pranayama means to get out of the way of the natural flow of life energy. Typically, it is stress, negative thinking, memories, and emotions that short-circuit our breathing.

Some types of breathing are stimulating, or "pranic"—imagine panting or roaring like a lion. Other types are calming, like sighing or taking long, slow exhales. Generally it is a good idea to learn pranayama with a teacher, because it does have an effect on your nervous system, and it can be unsettling or anxiety-inducing if practiced without some introductory knowledge. Once you have learned the basics, pranayama can be a rewarding and satisfying tool for soothing body and mind.

Practice & Reflect

Breathing practice:

- Find a private place where you can make a little noise without feeling self-conscious. Recline in a chair or lie down on the floor.
- Close your eyes (or use an eye pillow), and lightly block your ears with your fingers.
- Take a deep inhale through your nostrils, and then as you exhale make a humming sound. The pitch you choose does not matter as long as it's comfortable and easy to produce.
- When you run out of breath on the exhale, inhale through the nose and repeat.
- Continue for at least twelve breaths and then rest.

- This technique is called Brahmari or "Bee's Breath" and it is helpful for calming the nervous system. I also like to use it (minus the closed eyes and ears) when driving in stressful situations like winter white-outs or heavy rainstorms.

Beauty, Health, and Wabi-sabi

Beauty is the harvest of presence.
— David Whyte

One of the best things about a committed yoga practice (with attention to all eight limbs) is that it stretches our minds as much as our hamstrings. Meditation allows us to see, eventually, the places where we're stuck. It's a practice that takes us through the looking glass, once we get past the obstacle of our own reflection. Many of our deepest and most treasured beliefs are not of our own making. We absorb them by osmosis, because our culture steeps us in them. If you live your life immersed in purple dye, eventually you'll turn purple.

The way we understand health and beauty is deeply impacted by the time and place we live in—and it is changeable. In the Renaissance, plump and pear-shaped was the ideal for women, in the 1960s it was twig-thin, in the 1990s it was Loni Anderson (tiny waist, huge boobs), and according to the health magazine I just looked at, being "super-fit" is now the epitome of beauty. No matter what the trend, the common thread is that the "ideal" is unattainable for the majority of us. (And yes, men are in the same boat, but with slightly different criteria.)

So why do we torture ourselves? We don't do it to ourselves consciously; we just absorb the messages. Everywhere we look we see images of what is deemed desirable, placed there by individuals and companies that want to sell us the means to look more like the photos. The media depend on ad revenue from these companies to keep them in business, so they write articles to further the agenda of the lipstick-maker or the detox-purveyor. We all desperately want to feel loved and accepted, and we fall prey to the "experts" who tell us how to get there. And if you're over fifty, it's over. The only images of older people we ever see in North American magazines are of the super-fit, wrinkle-free, wealthy, air-brushed variety. This is starting to change, as marketers recognize that the older generations are far more prosperous than the younger—, but even so, the images we see set the bar impossibly high.

A few years ago, at a talk on Japanese Buddhist poetry, I learned about an esthetic called wabi-sabi. It is a view of beauty that accepts transience and imperfection. Richard Powell describes it as a view that "nurtures all that is authentic by acknowledging three simple realities: nothing lasts, nothing is finished, and nothing is perfect."[5] Wabi-sabi elevates that which is worn, simple, humble, or cracked. It appreciates determination and persistence in the face of obstacles and the ravages of time. It can look, really look, at a ninety-year-old face and celebrate the complex multifaceted being who has survived those nine decades. Wabi-sabi privileges what is real over what is ideal.

Our ideas about what aging means are what stop us from appreciating the beauty, the possibility, and the joy in it. We don't need to flagellate ourselves or pretend that aging isn't happening to us. We can learn to appreciate the esthetic of wabi-sabi and recognize the deeper beauty of presence, service, and the passage of time.

Practice & Reflect

Journal:

- When you hear the word beauty, who or what comes to mind?
- How do you feel about aging and beauty?

Beginner's Mind

In the beginner's mind there are many possibilities.
In the expert's mind there are few.
— Shunryu Suzuki

Becoming a yoga teacher can take the joy out of practicing yoga. Rather than fully relaxing into breath and movement, my brain is always grasping and churning: How can I teach this feeling? How can I translate this instruction to my class? How can I incorporate this movement into a different sequence?

In a world that is enamored with the "expert," we're all driven to pile on courses, certifications, and experiences. But expertise can come with a set of blinders. Teachers can forget what it feels like to not know something. I know a teacher who makes it her practice to always be studying something new and foreign to her everyday life. She says it helps her to be aware of what it feels like to be a new student in her class, aware of the feelings of fear, excitement, and maybe of not fitting in.

Not-knowing is a fertile cognitive field, but it's uncomfortable. I always find learning something new both fascinating and scary. The potential for missteps and embarrassment is high. My identity as "a person who knows" goes out the window, and I feel ungrounded.

At least once a year, my husband and I head to Quebec for a cycling trip. My command of Québècois is pretty poor, and in rural areas, there's no guarantee that anyone will be able to speak English. We struggle by, often receiving confused looks from hoteliers and waiters—but communication happens, humorous events ensue, and people are generous and kind. On the whole it's invigorating, and each year I learn a few more useful phrases, and get a little bolder in my attempts to communicate.

The beginner's mind is by definition an open mind. Beginners are often more creative problem-solvers, because they don't know that something (supposedly) can't be done. Or often, they accidentally do the un-doable, or create something that's never been made before. Furthermore, they haven't yet developed the habitual short-cuts that most of us take. They still have the excitement and enthusiasm that in those more experienced tends to atrophy with repetition.

There is nothing wrong with expertise and hard-won experience, and if you make an effort you can also maintain a beginner's mind. Beginner's mind is the state of suspending habit and egoic patterns in the face of whatever is arising at the moment. And beginner's mind can be a joyful and happy place.

In Buddhist texts, the most enlightened teachers may retire to gardening or disappear into obscurity. Achievement for them has become a distraction, and a diversion from their true path, which is to be fully present and absorbed in whatever they happen to be doing. If we let go of our ideas of self-importance, it's possible to take great satisfaction in washing a window or cleaning a bathroom. We can approach each experience as if we're doing it for the first time. When we let go of our imaginary, but deeply engrained system of weighing and measuring our value, something deep inside can finally relax and enjoy the tiny, beautiful things—like the hummingbird hovering at the feeder, or a delicious cup of coffee, or a beautifully rendered phrase.

Practice & Reflect

Think of an activity you do, or something you would like to try, that makes you feel like a beginner.

Looking Through a Longer Lens

Everywhere is within walking distance if you have the time.
— Steven Wright

Sunday evening I stayed up (too late) watching a documentary about Muhammad Ali. I read about him years ago in *Time*, and I remember him being controversial and arrogant, but I had no sense, back then, of the context of his behavior. The biopic was fascinating, because I realized that to understand Mohammed Ali, you have to understand the civil rights movement, Martin Luther King, Malcolm X, and the Vietnam War. When all of the social and cultural factors come into view (and only after many years have passed), Muhammad Ali comes out looking like a hero, and not the villain he was portrayed as for years.

I've been talking to friends lately about how to let go of things (and if you know me you'll laugh, because I'm not good at it). My dad's advice has always been to take a longer view. This requires some imagination, but it's not impossible. When we're in the midst of a break-up or a bad relationship or even just an annoying health problem, it feels insurmountable; it feels like we will suffer forever. What we fail to account for is time passing. The saying "Time heals everything" applies in most cases, but we can't wrap our heads around this simple truth. Nothing is permanent. We have to zoom out with the lens of our attention if we want to let something go. We have to imagine who we will be in twenty years' time, to step back from our sense of self-importance. No matter how successful or fit or attractive we are, we're all going to die in the end. We are just one of nearly eight billion individuals trying to make our way in the world. All of our lives are set within much larger social and cultural currents that we can't see (like fish in water), and the ideas we grasp for, the stories we cling to, are largely imaginary. Some are bizarre, like the notion that Donald Trump is a model of success. If we can imagine a wider view, a longer view, we can see that carrying an extra ten pounds, or not getting along with a co-worker, or missing out on a promotion, are all pretty small things in the end. Our feelings still hurt, and we need to acknowledge our pain, but we don't need to obsess over it. That way we can save our energy, focus on writing new stories, and create new possibilities for making the best use of the short time we have.

Practice & Reflect

Journal:

- Write about a situation that is irksome to you today.
- Then imagine time-traveling ten years into the future. Looking "backward," imagine some ways the situation could have been resolved.
- Reflect on whether any of the imagined solutions could be implemented or started here and now.

Part Seven: Equanimity

Hope is not the conviction that something will turn out well, but the certainty it is worth doing no matter how it turns out.
— Vaclav Havel

We've arrived at the last phase of our journey (although in truth, these steps don't really happen in order, and our progress is not apt to be linear). We might think of these stages or ideals as familiar landmarks that we encounter and recognize more readily the longer we've been on the road.

Sometimes identified as a state of happiness, equanimity is the ability to take the good with the bad. It's the place we arrive at when we stop trying to control everything. It represents the capacity to surf life's ups and downs, without becoming overwhelmed, cynical or angry.

The state of equanimity is a paradox: the holding of opposites that are both true. We are realistic and honest about what is happening in the world, but we don't act out in fear or anger, and we don't blame or shame. Like the goddess of compassion, Kuan Yin, we listen to the cries of the world even when powerless to do anything about them. Kuan Yin collects tears in a vase and pours them back into the ocean.

I've found the last three years incredibly challenging. All of my ideals about how things should be in the world have been exploded. At the time of life when I've finally got my shit more or less together, the environment, democracy, and social cohesion are falling to pieces. Racism, sexism, nastiness, and misinformation flow across my Twitter feed like a scene from an Orwellian nightmare.

A few months ago I read an essay by Daisy Hernandez on equanimity,[1] which I highly recommend. Within the essay she references a quote by African-American writer James Baldwin:

> It began to seem that one would have to hold in the mind forever two ideas which seemed to be in opposition. The first idea was acceptance, totally without rancor, of life as it is, and men as they are: in the light of this idea it goes without saying that injustice is a commonplace. But this did not mean that one could be complacent, for the second idea was of equal power: that one must never, in one's own life, accept these injustices as commonplace but must fight them with all one's strength. This fight begins, however, in the heart and it now had been laid to my charge to keep my own heart free of hatred and despair.[2]

The hygiene and maintenance of our hearts is the ultimate task, and gift, of equanimity. It requires focus, mindfulness, effort, ethics, joy, and enough spaciousness and relaxation to escape from the treadmill of habit.

We can work toward equanimity, or we can hope that with age and experience, equanimity will come to us. I think that it can happen either way, or both ways. The essays that follow explore ways we can achieve acceptance, while remaining engaged, active, and fully alive.

Practice & Reflect

Journal:

- Reflect on a hot-button issue that you are passionate about.
- Who are the "players" involved in this issue who provoke you?
- How do you manage or prevent feelings of "hatred and despair" in your heart?

A Trinity of Practices

The Buddhist word for wisdom, prajna, is often defined by Zen teachers as "before knowing." This type of wisdom values curiosity and openness more than acquisition.
— Ethan Nichtern

Years ago I attended an urban retreat in Toronto with the Buddhist teacher Bernie Glassman. On the Friday night he spoke on stage at University of Toronto's Hart House. He was a small, grey-haired man who made his way to the microphone wearing jeans, a plaid shirt, and a clown nose. Although he had excelled in the world of academia, and was an aeronautical engineer with a PhD in mathematics as well as a Zen teacher, he had chosen to leave the monastery to work on the streets of New York City.

Glassman had made it his mission to end homelessness in New York. He knew it was impossible, and still he made it his life's work. He started an organization called the Zen Peacemakers. One of his first projects was building a for-profit brownie factory and hiring people who had failed at all other kinds of employment: ex-prisoners, drug addicts, and mentally ill homeless people.

When he spoke with us, his primary theme was interdependence. He used his body as an analogy. He said, when we cut our right hand, our left hand jumps immediately into action to staunch the bleeding. It doesn't think about it or debate whether the right hand was worthy. When one part of our body suffers, the whole body suffers. When one part of the human race suffers, the whole is diminished.

Bernie's meditation retreats often took place in the streets of New York, or sometimes on the grounds outside Auschwitz. He summarized his key practices as the trinity of bearing witness, not-knowing, and compassionate action. Bearing witness means using some of our most precious resources—attention, focus, and time—in the service of those who suffer. Most poignantly, many of Bernie's students who practiced living on the streets reported that the most challenging part of the assignment was not facing the hunger or the cold (although that was extremely difficult), but the fact that passersby refused to look at them. They felt less than human.

Since that time, I've made it a practice to look into the eyes of beggars and the homeless, and it is an uncomfortable thing to do. Painful, because that connection, however brief, makes me feel their suffering. Even more painful because I see all the ways that I resist doing anything about it. I feel my reluctance to give them money, even though I have plenty of money. I feel my repulsion if they smell bad, my fear if they are behaving strangely, and most of all, my tidy, guilt-free world rubbing up against inequality and injustice.

Bearing witness is really uncomfortable and challenging, so why do it?

Because it matters. We are a species deeply wired to need contact. We learn to know ourselves in part as we are reflected in the eyes of others. Shunning and solitary confinement are punishments precisely because they separate us from the life-blood of connection.

As I struggled through the various crises in my life, what got me through were the people in my life willing to sit down and hold the space for me to say what I needed to say, even if it was self-centered or ridiculous. In fact, we value this so highly that those who can afford to do so pay psychotherapists healthy chunks of money to do it for us. As we air our grievances and our pain, our witnesses mirror, console, and provide different perspectives—and these small things (which are in fact big things) can save us from ourselves.

To truly bear witness, we need to step away from fixing, teaching, and knowing. This differentiates bearing witness from therapy or interference. In my own life, in times of distress, I don't find it helpful to be told that God will take care of it. That statement and other variations on that theme shut down witnessing. It closes the door to discomfort, which is also the door to relationship and interdependence. Not-knowing means to step out of the comforts of storytelling, advice giving, and cliché. It means not defaulting to "The government should look after this." Not-knowing is a strange and uncomfortable place to live—but it's also the vacuum that invites in creativity and imagination. It's the place where new ideas and insights can germinate.

The third step, according to Glassman, is compassionate action, which arises automatically from bearing witness and not-knowing, and is not the product of think-tanks or moralists or religious ideals. Compassionate action grows out of empathy and may not match the expected narrative about the right thing to do—for example, giving an opium addict methadone. Methadone doesn't fix the addiction, but it may mean that the individual doesn't have to sell his body to get a fix. It doesn't remedy his low self-esteem, but it gives him a choice. It doesn't seek to change who he is.

Michael once told me that the role of the teacher is to mirror the students back to themselves. This is a humbling idea, because no matter how much status or knowledge you accumulate, the real test of your skill is your capacity for empathy—your capacity to get out of your habits and your knowledge and into the scary arena of really letting somebody in. It takes immense courage not only to feel and witness your own vulnerability but also to fully bear witness to someone else's.

Bernie Glassman passed away last year after suffering a debilitating stroke, but his organization, the Zen Peacemakers, is alive and well.[3]

Practice & Reflect

Bearing witness challenge:

- Many of us stay comfortable by avoiding or disengaging from issues. One way to work with this is to bracket a specific amount of time to witness and learn about things we'd rather not know about. If you don't bother watching the news, a good practice would be to purchase and read a reputable paper for a week. Or, if there is an issue that speaks to you, like hunger or homelessness, take a few hours to research and educate yourself about what's going on in your community. Perhaps even go and visit a food bank or homeless shelter. You don't have to commit to volunteering, but at least speak to some of the people there. Find out what the needs are, even if you're not in the position to help right now.

"There's a Starman Waiting in the Sky"

Check ignition, and may God's love be with you.
— David Bowie, "Space Oddity" (Tweeted by the Vatican when David Bowie died)

It's official. I'm haunted.

As a life-long fan, I was delighted that Bowie released a new album on his birthday, and then was stunned to learn of his death two days later. As music journalist Alan Cross so aptly stated, "David Bowie [was] not supposed to die."[4] Bowie was king of the freaks and the misfits: fearless, androgynous, shape-shifting, enigmatic. He had strange eyes, bad teeth (until the 1980s), and a powerful command of uncanny symbolism. He was a charismatic artist in every sense of the word. He unnerved us, challenged us, and demanded that we step out of our comfortable worldview. He was also a fallible human being who spent much of the 1970s junked-out on cocaine and heroin, but thankfully he came out the other side. By all accounts in recent years he had focused on a quiet life with his family, and was a kind and generous friend.

His last video, "Lazarus," was electrifying. I have no idea if he knew that he would be comatose by the time it was released—that he would literally be performing a message from beyond the grave about a man who came back from the dead. This video is magnetic, shocking in its honesty, and a fusion of all Bowie's exceptional talents. He was a master of non-verbal communication. He had trained in mime and worked as an actor both on Broadway and in film.

"Lazarus" is Bowie contemplating his own death, and he doesn't prettify or romanticize it. His lyrics ("*Look up here, I'm in heaven*") are at once deeply personal, elliptical, and sometimes ironic ("*Everybody knows me now*"). The female figure of death (or love, or both) comes out of the closet, and from under the bed, like a childhood monster. The deceased character in the bed wears a death mask, while the "live" Bowie, dressed in a jumpsuit that combines "prisoner" and "clown," frantically tries to get more writing done in between moments of fear and anxiety. This is a character who is not at peace, not ready to die, and Bowie is fearless about letting us see that. No one has ever created anything vaguely like this, and he took as great a risk with his swan song as he did when he first took to the stage as Ziggy Stardust. He makes us look at our own mortality by allowing us to glimpse his.

According to the yoga sutras, one of the obstacles to our liberation from suffering is *abhinivesa*, which translates as "fear of death" or "fear of letting go of the story of me." Patanjali wrote that "clinging to life is instinctive and self-perpetuating, even for the wise."[5] In other words, it's normal to be afraid of this great unknown, but whether we're afraid or not, all of us have to let go.

Shunryu Suzuki said, "Things teach best when they're dying."[6] Of course, we're all dying, we just don't want to think about it. For me David Bowie was the embodiment of creative possibility who always seemed a little ethereal, alien, and impossible to know—which is true of all of us. We're constantly shifting and changing as the conditions around us change. We can never entirely know one another or ourselves, because we are deeply ephemeral beings. David Bowie understood that and lived it. And now he is gone, and not gone. Here, and not here. He has taken his greatest leap, and "Just like that bluebird," he is free.

He always blew my mind, and I'm grateful for his legacy.

Practice & Reflect

Journal:

- What fears come to mind when you think about dying?
- How could you respond to them productively? Are there actions you could take now, such as updating your will, that would give you more peace of mind?

To Thine Own Self Be True

*From the sea of effortlessness, let your great uncaused
compassion shine forth.*
— Hakuin Ekaku

The problem with any tradition that lays out a path, that ponders meaning, ethics, and all of those good things, is that in the end, no one can tell you what to do. This path toward awakening starts with the assumption that you're perfect just the way you are, *and* that you could use a little improvement. But what improvement means, well, that's up to you. Trying to figure out those essential questions—Who am I? What should I be when I grow up? Why am I here?—it's a life's work, and there may never be an answer. Maybe all that soul-searching is reduced to declarations or aspirations. Getting comfortable with not trying so hard is also a prospect on the path to equanimity.

We are defined by the choices we make day after day, and the choices we make are dependent on hundreds of other moving pieces. Entering the arena of yoga to explore some of these pieces is a choice—and one that can stretch you in every dimension. But unlike most of the other self-improvement projects we take on, this path asks you to stop trying to get somewhere. Instead, we're working on getting truly intimate with what's happening right now, how we're behaving in this moment, what's pulling us, what's pushing us. We're trying to get away from planning and back to what's honest and elemental.

Unfortunately, yoga and meditation have become entwined with the self-improvement industry. It's not unexpected or unnatural that a spiritual path has had a one-night stand with capitalism and produced a baby that no one is confident about parenting. Certainly some good things have come of the union: what used to be esoteric and available only in India has become a worldwide phenomenon, and modern medicine has been able to make postural practice safer as well as contribute scientific research into why and how the practices work. But there are issues too, including sexual abuse by teachers, cultural appropriation, body-shaming, and an editing-out of many of the teachings (at times for the better, at times for the worse). It's almost impossible to say what's truly yoga and what isn't. The ground is shifting, and people will keep arguing about what's essential until we go extinct, which is, for me anyway, a more pressing issue.

The shift away from spiritual aspects of the teachings toward self-improvement seems a misdirection. The self-help world has an underlying drive to perfectibility that can lead directly into more suffering, rather than out of it. Which is not to say that self-help is not useful to people, just that it operates on a different principle. The goal of self-help is usually happiness, while the goal of the spiritual path is freedom and knowing one's true nature. The freedom yogis strive for is from illusion, fear, and ego-identification. The ego is the self-improvement director, and can only look at things from a narrow perspective. Freedom, in yoga, comes from recognizing that the true nature of the self is much larger, more fluid, and more whole than anything the ego can imagine.

I found *Promise Land,* Jessica Lamb-Shapiro's book about the self-help industry, insightful and enlightening. In her research she examined both the pros and cons of self-help and the cultural framework that it embraces. She says, "As Americans, self-help reflects our core beliefs: self-reliance, social mobility, an endless ability to overcome obstacles, a fair and equal pursuit of success, and the inimitable proposition that every single human wants and deserves a stack of cash. An ideology that reflects what you already believe is bound to make you feel validated"[7] Self-help can allow us to feel less alone and isolated, but it also tends to minimize or dismiss real-world obstacles like poverty, discrimination, mental illness, or other forms of structural inequality. Self-help is usually about winning an imagined lottery and getting all the things we believe we want: an adoring family, friends, an ageless body, a vacation property, and the ability to be generous to causes we care about. Self-help is useful for developing better life skills, and we need healthy boundaries and self-respect to function well in the world. But it all comes down to fulfilling egoic needs.

In yoga the ego is sometimes called the *ahamkara*, or I-maker; it's the storyteller that makes us feel coherent and stable. But it can overstep, and doesn't necessarily see things as they really are. Our egoic self is influenced by all kinds of needs and desires: to fit in, to be loved, to feel productive, to be seen. The poor dear can be yanked around easily by other people's agendas, by other people's stories.

Freedom, in yoga, is what's left when we let go of our illusions about being separate, permanent, or trapped by our past. Freedom means that we take ourselves less seriously, and become better at being patient and kind. Zen teachers often say that the meaning of enlightenment is "an appropriate response"—that is, the ability to be fully present, free of the fetters of our ideas, social standing, or future planning, and to respond fully and spontaneously from a place of openness and connection. It's a mind-set that we can't get to by thinking. We arrive only by stripping away the layers of self until we hit curiosity.

If you take this too literally, you could argue that the state of freedom corresponds to something like dementia, in which the markers of personhood, like memory and relationship, are lost. That's going too far. Freedom is about being able to step outside yourself for a moment; it's not a dissociative state, but rather a flexibility superpower. It's knowing you can let go if you want to. And like the mother who lifts a car off a child in a panic, or the hero who runs into a burning building to rescue a child, something bigger, more ancient, and more all-encompassing takes over when we temporarily forget ourselves. Yet as the title of Jack Kornfield's well-known book points out, *After the Ecstasy, the Laundry*. "Freedom is a place we can visit, but we're still humans living a human life. We still need to cook dinner, pay our bills, and floss our teeth."[8]

In the end, whoever you are, however you experience yourself to be is just a nexus of conditions (time, place, memories, who you're with); and whatever the sum of that is—is. You can only do one moment at a time, and do your best with your own feelings and judgments in that moment. Your best self is what you already are right now, not some pending possibility. You should listen, and keep an open mind, but mainly, to thine own self be true.

Practice & Reflect

Journal:

- Are there aspects of yourself you hide from others?
- Do you go on self-improvement jags? If so, what are the areas you feel need to be improved?
- What gets in the way of accepting yourself as you are now?

BE KIND TO YOURSELF

*Meditation requires patience and maitri. If this process
of clear-seeing isn't based on self-compassion it will
become a process of self-aggression.*
— Pema Chödrön

Whatever spiritual yellow brick road we find ourselves following, we all have a tendency to judge ourselves against some imagined ideal. The more capacity we have for introspection, the more likely we'll feel unworthy, or hopeless, or frustrated with our lack of "progress." Even if we're committed to not going anywhere, we can still be upset with our anger, our habits, or our tendency to judge others. My personal example is the fact that I can still be moved to rage by telemarketers, or big game hunters posing with dead animals on Facebook.

In Buddhism there is a practice called maitri (m-uh-y-tree), which means self-directed compassion or loving-kindness. It's not the same as self-esteem, which involves self-worth and egoic functions like boundary-setting or asking for what we need. Self-compassion means you nurture your ability to be with your pain, your failures, and your bad habits without shame, blame, or beating yourself up. Although you may be a mess, you recognize that you still deserve kindness and dignity, and you stop trying to disown parts of yourself so you can become something you think is better. Instead of beating yourself up, you turn your focus to curiosity, patience, and self-acceptance.

Maitri may be another way of framing what used to be called "inner child" work. You imagine the part of you that is suffering is young and unformed, in need of care, reassurance, and kindness. We all have far more ease accepting a young child who needs comforting than we do an adult in the same emotional space. We can love children without expecting them to be other than they are.

Self-compassion takes time and effort to develop, and meditation practice is a good place to work with it. When we're learning to meditate, one of the first steps, aside from concentrating, is learning to stay with whatever we're feeling, especially if it's unpleasant (e.g., embarrassment, shame, or anger). Allowing and investigating uncomfortable emotions is a first step toward processing them. One tool I find particularly helpful is to focus on where in my body I'm actually sensing whatever I'm feeling; for example, sadness feels like a heavy swelling somewhere behind the inner point of my eyebrows. The point of exploring in this way is not to "fix" or eliminate the feeling, but rather to experience it fully, with curiosity and willingness. Often if you stay with a feeling, you'll notice that it shifts. Sometimes it even departs.

When we are toddlers, we learn to control our emotions and impulses as our brains develop the capacity to do so. Otherwise, we'd still be having two-year-old meltdowns at age forty at the grocery store checkout. Emotional regulation is needed for us to have relationships with other people. The down side is that sometimes during this process, we become afraid of our emotions and fear we'll be shamed, punished, or isolated if we don't control them enough. We look to our models for what is acceptable, and in some cultures we see stoicism and a "stiff upper lip." Some of us become disembodied and unable to identify or connect with our feelings. What gets lost is the inherent wisdom that emotions contain, and along with that, our ability to be intimate emotionally with others. Love gets lost.

Our emotions live in a different part of the brain than our executive functions—which include the planner, the pleaser, and the judge. Emotions operate at a level that is non-verbal and in the background to thinking, but they have important things to tell us. We like to talk about our hearts and minds as if they have separate functions, but they can't be separated. Our thinking processes affect our feelings in myriad ways. We can inflate or repress what we're feeling through such activities as storytelling, rationalizing, and imagining, with all the mental processes at our disposal. Similarly, thinking, such as obsessing about anxiety-provoking issues like climate change, can wreak havoc on our emotions. The assignment in practicing maitri is to experience a feeling without adding anything—not even a name. We stop, we sit, and we hold its hand, but otherwise leave it alone. This type of practice can shift our consciousness profoundly, like the movement of underground tectonic plates.

Another aspect of working with emotions is learning not to identify with them so much. We can expand our understanding of what emotions signify. Emotions aren't necessarily personal—they're embodied states mitigated by neurochemicals, genetics, memories, cultural norms, and countless other factors. They don't necessarily "belong" to us. Emotions are an energetic "language" that we share with all humans, and, as we are learning, with some animal species as well. Emotions can be inflamed and preyed upon by marketers, politicians, and Twitter trolls, or they can be used to move people to care for themselves and others.

Self-compassion means that when we're feeling difficult things, we treat ourselves with tenderness, even if we've done something wrong or stupid We don't absolve ourselves or avoid responsibility, we just recognize that we deserve kindness and compassion as much as the next person. Moving on, atoning, and making amends are rooted in self-compassion. We can't extend forgiveness or kindness to others until we learn to extend it to ourselves.

Practice & Reflect

Journal:

- Imagine a ritual that you could undertake when you find yourself in need of self-compassion. It could be something as simple as taking a hot bath or going for a walk. Write it down.

- Or, imagine someone who is dealing with the same difficulties you are, and then write a letter of support. Mail it to yourself.

Your Gifts Will Bring You Home

Once upon a time there was a young girl named Clare, who was born within the walls of an ancient and beautiful city called Oceania. Located on the shore of a turquoise sea, it was surrounded by a fragrant and impenetrable jungle. Its gardens were walled with moss-covered stone, and fountains plashed in ponds bordered by lotus flowers. But Clare's parents were young and adventurous, eager to travel and see new sights. So the family moved far away to the land of Pangura, to seek their fortunes and explore other cultures.

Soon after, misfortune befell them. The settlement they had chosen was invaded. The adults were slaughtered, and the children taken away to work as domestics and slaves. Clare, although heartbroken, was one of the lucky ones. She was sent to live with a kind, elderly woman, who taught her to grow medicines, read the stars, and navigate with a compass. After a few years, Clare's benefactor fell ill and worried about whether Clare could survive on her own. Clare had many talents and skills, but none that would serve her well in Pangura.

Late one night, she summoned Clare to her bedside and said, "It is time for you to make your way back home. When I am gone, there will be nothing for you here. I will give you all the money I can spare, and you must take this compass, and trust in it no matter what happens."

It was an odd compass, marked with an "O" where the "N" should have been, but Clare received it with gratitude.

"Go now, my child, before the night watch begins, and carry me in your heart."

Clare was afraid, but did as she was directed to do. Within hours of her escape from Pangura, she stumbled into a crevice and woke up in a cave guarded by an Ogre.

He said, "I will shelter and protect you, but in return you must fill out these forms from dawn to dusk, and you must convince people to purchase my potions, and you must cook for me and do my laundry."

Clare complied for a time, but she longed for Oceania, and she ran away so many times that the Ogre grew tired of the exercise and finally agreed to let her go.

He was angry and disappointed that she was so ungrateful, but on the day of her departure, he called her aside and said, "I fear that your wrongheadedness and stupidity will get you killed, but you have served me well. I offer you this gift. It came to me from my father and is precious to me." And he handed her a dusty, cat-shaped figurine made of jade.

She thanked him and set out on her way.

Clare wandered for days in the dense forests, checking the compass (that pointed to "O" for Oceania) as she scrambled through brambles. She often thought about jettisoning the jade ornament, but she kept it and struggled on, surviving on wild berries and leaves.

One day she came upon a broken man. He had fallen down at the side of the trail and was too weak to get up again. She brought him food, dressed his wounds with salves, and built a shelter to keep him out of the rain and cold. Gradually he healed, and she readied him for her departure.

As she packed her few belongings, he came to her, holding a small, weather-beaten journal. "I have nothing of value to give you," he said, "but this book belonged to my mother, and it is precious to me. Please take it with you, and remember my gratitude when you read it."

The words and symbols in the book were ornate and beautiful, but Clare couldn't make head nor tail of them. She accepted his gift gratefully and tucked it into her backpack.

Many days later, having followed the compass into a desert, she stopped at an oasis that was occupied by a tribe of elephants and a handsome prince. She was immediately smitten. The prince was generous and kind, and invited her into his court. She found it a joyous place and felt genuinely at home there. He was betrothed to another, but he and Clare loved each other in their harmless way. She taught him what she knew of medicinal herbs and how to read the stars, and he taught her the art of stillness and listening, and shared ancient teachings from his kingdom. Before his wedding, she used the last of her money to buy him and his bride a golden bowl. In return he gave her a beautiful vase, filled with saltwater, and sealed with a cork.

He said, "This was given to me by a traveling monk from Oceania, and it is extremely precious to me. I trust that someday you will know what to do with it."

Not long after the wedding, a dark lord invaded the palace and murdered the prince along with several of his courtiers. As she stood brokenhearted beside the funeral pyres, Clare resolved that she must continue on her journey.

After countless grueling days and nights, she despaired of ever making it home and began to wonder if the compass was leading her astray. She was thin, malnourished, and so very tired. She feared that by the time she made it back to Oceania, it might be totally changed or even unwelcoming.

At long last she drew closer to the walls of the city, but found them impenetrable. She struggled through thick undergrowth, scraping her thin knees and aching body. After two long days she came to a guardhouse, but found it occupied by an angry witch who declared, "No one shall pass!" Clare pleaded with her and argued with her, and tried to overpower her, but to no avail.

Finally Clare slumped down beside the witch's door and sobbed until she was so empty that she cared not whether she lived or died. As she sat there in a reverie, remembering all she had lost and all she had been through, the witch cleared her throat and spoke.

"When I was a young girl, about your age, I was condemned to this outpost by an evil queen. She was as beautiful as she was wicked, and she disposed of all who opposed her. My sisters and I went to battle against her, but her magic was subtle and sinister, and our own people betrayed us. I cannot let you into the city any more than I can let myself out of this prison."

Clare sat up against the wall and riffled through the items in her backpack.

"Perhaps," she said, "to pass the time you could read me something from this book," and she handed her the notebook from the fallen man. "I cannot understand the language, but maybe you can."

The witch gasped and turned the pages hungrily. "This is a grimoire, a book of spells!" She studied it carefully, and a few hours later turned to Clare and said, "Fetch me some bridle-vine, a milkweed pod, and a round stone."

Clare stumbled off into the forest and did her bidding. It took several days to find all three items, but find them she did.

The witch placed the items on a small altar, and said, "I know this seems impossible, but now I need jade and a vase full of tears."

Clare rummaged through her pack and handed her the jade cat from the Ogre and the saltwater from the Prince. The witch placed the cat on the altar and poured the saltwater all around, while intoning a solemn chant from the grimoire. The ground trembled, and stones began tumbling down all around the guardhouse. In the midst of the rubble was a tarnished brass key.

The witch had been transfigured. She still looked old, but everything about her features had softened and opened. She nodded to Clare to take the key. Clare inserted it carefully into the gate that had appeared there, the lock clanked, and the door groaned open.

Oceania lay before her, beautiful, verdant, and warm, just the way she remembered it.

Coping with Grief

Why is the measure of love loss?
— Jeanette Winterson

Grief is one of life's inevitable truths. All of us will experience it, and it will change us. When someone we love dies, a part of us dies with them. The word *bereaved* means "to be torn." We will never be the same again. And no matter what we believe about what happens next, our loved ones who have gone beyond cannot be reached for comment.

Death is not cognitively comprehensible. Our loved ones are not here, but they live on in our memories and in our bodies and minds. Energy is neither created nor destroyed, according to the laws of physics. I really don't know what happens after we die, but I'm open to any possibility.

One way of thinking about it was expressed beautifully by John Donne in his poem "A Valediction Forbidding Mourning":

> Our two souls therefore, which are one,
> Though I must go, endure not yet
> A breach, but an expansion,
> Like gold to airy thinness beat.

In other words, the loss is not an ending, but merely a change to something more spacious, something bigger. He goes on to compare the two lovers to the two points of a compass, still tethered mystically together. And if we think of our interconnectedness with every molecule, every element, every life force on the planet, it's impossible that we could ever be truly alone. We all live on in each other.

As Sheryl Sandberg said after the sudden loss of her husband in 2015, "I think when tragedy occurs it presents a choice. You can give in to the void, the emptiness that fills your heart, your lungs, constricts your ability to think or even breathe. Or you can try to find meaning."[9]

Here is what I've learned from my own grief, and what I need to tell myself over and over:

- *It helps to be friendly toward the pain.* Don't try to be okay. Cry with abandon. Or don't. Do what you need to do.

- *Remember that loss is not personal.* Nor is it punishment. It's just life doing what life does. Death touches us all, no matter how good we are, no matter how important we are. Try not to feed your pain with stories of guilt and self-recrimination.

- *This doesn't have to pervade every aspect of your existence.* It's okay to laugh. It's okay to spend a day at the gym. It's okay to live your life. That's what your loved one would want for you.

- *Everything is impermanent.* You won't feel like this forever. You just have to trust in time.

- *Reflect on the joy and happiness that this person brought to your life.* Focus on how lucky you were to have known them.

- *Bundle up all the love you have for the person you've lost, and give it to somebody else.*

As we get older, the capacity to deal with grief becomes one of our most important skills. Losing people we love can leave us feeling as if we have a hole in our heart. The question is, what comes through the hole? Can we use it to truck around a little more love and tenderness, or is it the passageway to what's dark and sad? It can be both, or neither. What makes the difference are the friends and family who gather round to help us through. All weights are lighter when they're shared.

Practice & Reflect

Journal:

- Write a letter to someone you are grieving. Decide what you would like to do with it, for example, you could keep it tucked under your meditation cushion, or share it with a close friend, or burn it. Choose something that feels safe and meaningful.

- If you're not comfortable writing, you could draw, paint, sing or otherwise express the emotions you're feeling.

Samsara and Its Antidotes

*If you cannot find peace within yourself,
you will never find it anywhere else.*
— Marvin Gaye

I'm in the midst of facilitating an online course on ethics, and woke up today to another news story that left me gutted. All week I've been contemplating what the Buddha referred to as the three poisons: greed, anger, and delusion. These mental attributes keep us trapped in "samsara," also known as "the cycle of meaningless, painful existence." They were concerns in the time of the Buddha, and are just as worrying today.[10]

In recent years greed seems to have become venerated by our culture. Obscene levels of wealth and conspicuous consumption are admired, and wealth has become confused with wisdom. We somehow accept that a tiny minority of people control the vast majority of the world's resources, and that there's nothing wrong with CEOs making hundreds of times what their workers make, or taking bonuses even as they bankrupt their companies. The spokes-model for anger has stepped onto the world stage and happily churns it up, misdirecting it at scapegoats; and delusion is propagated everywhere, by fake news writers, interest groups, and sadly, the White House. "Alternative facts" are offered even in the face of evidence to the contrary. It's enough to give a yogini a breakdown.

But before we can tackle greed, anger, and delusion in the world, we have to work with these negative attributes in our own hearts. We have to see how these mental states come up in our choices and in our actions. I actively struggle with them all, and I see them raise their ugly heads during my meditation practice. Mostly, they are rooted in fear.

Fortunately there are antidotes to the three poisons.

Generosity

The first antidote is to be as generous as our means permit. We actively work to balance self-care with caring for others and to appreciate the gifts we have been given (such as living in a safe haven with enough food) without clinging and allowing fear to cause us to take more than is necessary. Saving for a rainy day is wise, but no amount of money can save us from violent dictators or environmental disasters. Generosity can build communities and reduce the kinds of suffering we actually can do something about, like hunger or isolation. Generosity is the antidote to greed.

Loving-kindness

The second antidote is metta, or loving-kindness. When we can stop seeing people as ideas and concepts and instead see them as individuals with unique lives, it's possible to break through the anger. I heard an interview on CBC with a rancher whose property was being crossed every day by heavily armed drug runners. When I heard him speak, rationally, about how frightened he was and how worried he was about his children, I understood why he wants a wall. I'm not sure that a wall is the answer, but I can see a real person with a valid perspective trying to solve a problem in the best way he knows how. I can't be angry with him. Empathy (loving-kindness) is the antidote to anger.

Wisdom

The third antidote is wisdom. In the face of delusion and lies, we can educate ourselves, we can do research, we can support news organizations that have reporters who are accredited and trained, who have a code of ethics, and who support factual, unbiased journalism. As newspapers and news stations struggle to stay alive because of plummeting revenues, we need to step up our support. We need to care about whether what we read is true, and test it out for ourselves. Wisdom requires that we keep our minds open and be willing to be proved wrong. It requires a healthy degree of skepticism when browsing the internet.

Practice & Reflect

Generosity Practice:

- Choose either a person or a cause that you know is in need of assistance.
- Reach out with an offer of help or a donation.
- Observe how taking action makes you feel.
- If you can do this anonymously, notice how that feels.

Ten Characteristics of Resilient People

The last of human freedoms is one's ability to choose one's attitude in a given set of circumstances.
— Victor Frankl

Over my long career as an occupational therapist, I had the good fortune to meet many extraordinary people who were living with difficult illnesses, disabilities, or addictions. The resilient among them adapted extremely well and lived creative and fulfilling lives. Others suffered without reprieve. I've always been curious about the differences between those who thrived and those who just survived—or didn't.

The observations I share here are simplifications. Every person and situation is unique. And I'm not going to discuss the social determinants of health, such as wealth, stability, social support, or education. These factors make a huge difference, and no matter how amazing you are as a person, if you are poor or isolated, you will have a harder time of it. Also, research has demonstrated that people who suffer abuse or trauma in their early years will carry that with them. Even those who feel they've overcome childhood pain are more susceptible to illness than their peers who had happy, stable childhoods.

So how did some of these people exhibit resilience?

- They were able to focus on the present. They didn't spend a lot of time obsessing about the past and how things went wrong, or mourning the future that they had expected to have. Instead, they spent their energy on what they could still do.
- They didn't take their struggles personally. Yes, they may have had regrets (I wish I had never started smoking), but they recognized

that whatever happened to them was not a punishment or a failure. They let go of trying to know "why?" and focused on "what now?"

- They were open-minded and willing to try new methods of doing things. They were willing to change their habits if it meant improving their situation. They were clear about their values and priorities, but still willing to listen and negotiate.

- They were interested in learning, in current events, and in meeting and getting to know new people. They didn't become self-obsessed.

- They stayed focused, even when they ran into dead ends. They did not take no for an answer. For example, I met a fellow who engineered his own in-home elevator when he wasn't able to afford to buy one. All he needed was the idea. His able-bodied friends helped him build it.

- They combined problem-solving and imagination, accomplishing things that were creative and a little radical. I remember a woman who cut a hole in her bedroom wall so that she could watch her son play in the yard on days she was too weak to get up. Her priority was to be a mother first and house-proud second. She reasoned that the hole could be repaired, but neglecting the needs of her young son could not be.

- They exhibited optimism and humor. They were able to find a lighter side to life even in the darkest of moments. They were a joy to be around, which meant they attracted supportive friends and relatives. They also managed to find things to feel grateful about, even if it was only a set of fresh sheets, or a good movie on TV.

- They made an effort to keep relationships going. They would stay in touch with friends. They would volunteer, contribute, and listen even if they had extremely limited abilities. They were willing to be vulnerable and to experience and share their spectrum of emotions.

- Even if they had lost many of their abilities, they recognized that they had value and could still contribute, though not in the way they were used to. They did not blame themselves or others for their struggles—even when they legitimately could have.

- They had made their peace with death. They were still afraid, but also well aware that nobody gets out of here alive. Once they had accepted that they couldn't control the final act but could control their response to it, they seemed to be much lighter.

So what does this have to do with yoga?

The resilient people I came to know had all overcome what are known in yoga philosophy as the klesas, or "obstacles." These are:

Not seeing things as they really are.

Clinging to pleasure, and avoiding pain.

Getting caught up in egotism and stories about I, me, and mine, and not seeing that the sense of self is constantly in flux.

Fearing death, or rather fearing the "end of the story of me."

Resilient people are ordinary people who have come a long way toward overcoming these obstacles, and who, as a result, can cope with pain without becoming a slave to it. I was privileged to be able to witness and admire the qualities that made them who they were.

Practice & Reflect

Journal:

- Write about an event in your own life that caused you to need your resilience superpowers.
- Which of the examples above do you relate to?
- Are there skills you called on that aren't mentioned? If so, what were they?

Mono No Aware

The birds have vanished from the sky
and now the last cloud drains away.
We sit together the mountain and me,
until only the mountain remains.
— Li Bai

In Grade Eleven I took a course in World Religions that I wish would be compulsory for all humans. Not only did it open my mind to the diversity of belief systems and the roles religion plays in our societies, but it also highlighted the many ways in which various religions frame the same problems. Many share similar stories, but with different characters playing the principle roles.

Most religions address something that might be called the pain of self-awareness, which also includes awareness of our own mortality. Until recently, humans have claimed that the attribute that separates us from the animals is our capacity to be self-aware. (As an aside, current research on elephants and primates suggests that we may have been too quick to come to that conclusion.)

Self-awareness comes at a cost. As self-aware creatures, we know we are going to die, and we also know that we need to balance our needs with the needs of others. We know that we don't control the universe around us. We can be minding our own business walking down the street and be killed by a brick falling off a high-rise. Sometimes self-awareness is a buzzkill.

Religions address fears of mortality and loss. In fact, these two facts of life are probably the main reason we have religion—and, for that matter, philosophy. In Buddhism, recognition of impermanence is a central tenet.

As the saying goes, "We spend our lives with one foot in the grave and the other on a banana peel." No matter how well things are going, we will always have a little draft of sorrow sneaking in under the doorway of the house our self built.

The Old Testament frames this anxiety as a punishment from God for wanting to know too much. Everything was bliss in the Garden of Eden until Adam and Eve ate from the tree of knowledge of good and evil. The apple, the fruit of this tree, represented self-awareness. Once they'd eaten the apple, they realized their nakedness, their vulnerability, and that life from then on would be difficult. The "original sin" resulted in a separation from God and the safety and innocence of humanity's childhood. The struggle to survive would forever be a companion to selfhood. The development of meta-cognition (the ability to think about thinking) signals the end of childhood, and likewise, the moment Adam and Eve became self-aware, they were evicted from paradise.

We can distract ourselves from the awareness of impermanence. We can go about living our lives, accumulating things, numbing out, questing after fame or fortune. But no matter what we achieve, or who we vote for, or how many children we have, we're still going to die and eventually be forgotten.

And yet, even though we know this, life can still have so much joy in it.

The Japanese phrase "mono no aware" means "an awareness of impermanence, an empathy toward things, or a sensitivity to ephemera." It describes the wistfulness, or "gentle sadness," we feel about impermanence and the passage of time. The sadness will always be there in the background, even in the midst of joyful experiences. It's not depression, but rather a normal part of living a full and awakened life. It's the embodied feeling of impermanence—it's healthy and necessary.

Practice & Reflect

Journal:

- Think about times in your life when you've experienced mono no aware. Choose one and write it down.
- What feelings or images come to mind when you recall this event or moment in time?

The Brahmaviharas

To make things as easy as possible to understand, we can summarize the four boundless qualities in the single phrase "a kind heart." Just train yourself to have a kind heart always and in all situations.
— Patrul Rinpoche

The Four Brahmaviharas, or aspirations, are one of the many jewels of yoga that don't get a lot of airtime. They don't make for good Instagram posts, and repeated flowing sequences don't have a lot of impact on them. Nonetheless they are part of our yoga journey, if we're curious and open-minded.

The brahmaviharas show up in the Yoga Sutras (1.33) and also in Buddhist and pre-Buddhist texts (e.g., the Upanishads). They are behaviors we are meant to embody. The word *brahmavihara* translates into English as "abodes of the divine," but they are sometimes referred to as the four immeasurable or limitless qualities.

Metta

The first quality is *metta* and is translated as "loving-kindness." Metta takes work to develop, and this often means confronting our own emotional baggage. Traditional metta meditations start with cultivating loving-kindness toward ourselves, and then expanding the practice outward in ever-widening circles. When the Dalai Lama says "My religion is kindness," it is, in part, this practice he is referring to. Metta is the opposite of tribalism and requires a willingness to let go of our biases and prejudices. As much as we love our memes about kindness on Facebook, cultivating metta for people we don't like is demanding and difficult.

The facsimile of loving-kindness is attachment and self-involvement.[11] It might look the same from the outside, but it's contaminated by a desire to get something. For example, I will be kind as long as I get appreciation and rewards, and I will also demand that the recipient of my kindness behave the way I expect her to. The opposite of metta is hatred. We all know of people who get under our skin so completely that we can't abide even hearing their voice. This is where the hard work begins.

Maitri

The second brahmavihara is maitri, or compassion. Compassion means "to suffer with." To practice compassion means opening yourself up to intimacy and open-mindedness. It also means being willing to provide companionship and caring without judgment, and without ideas about "fixing" someone.

The facsimiles of compassion are pity, overwhelm, and idiot compassion. Pity implies looking down your nose at someone's pain from the safety of your secure and superior place in the world. Pity creates separation between you and the other. Overwhelm is the opposite: you become so enmeshed that you lose all perspective and thus your ability to be useful. Idiot compassion describes a situation where a well-meaning person showers love and limitless resources onto a person who repeatedly takes advantage of or abuses them. The opposite of compassion is cruelty: deliberately hurting someone.

Mudita

The third quality is *mudita*, and it means "to be joyful for someone else." Mudita is the feeling we experience when we witness a breathtaking Olympic performance, and we're thrilled for the athlete regardless of which country they came from. The "look-alike" of mudita is overexcitement or euphoric behavior. In the example above, that might translate into celebrity worship or stalking the athlete in question, which is delusional. In this case, the joyfulness has a clinginess to it and proliferates beyond the relevant moment. Living vicariously through others might be viewed as mudita gone awry. The opposite of mudita is envy. Rather than feeling happy for the other, we feel sad or angry that they have something we don't.

Upekkha

The word *upekkha* translates into English as equanimity, and means the ability to tolerate the ups and downs of life without clinginess or aversion. Equanimity requires both mental and emotional flexibility. When we're grief-stricken, we do the work of mourning. When we win the lottery, we recognize that money comes and goes, and it won't solve all of our problems. The false approximation of equanimity is indifference, or detachment. People who are nihilistic and say that nothing they do matters, or those who believe they've transcended the need to participate in relationships or worldly events, are caught up in the pretense of equanimity. The opposites of equanimity are prejudice, ideological rigidity, and fear. Equanimity is required to go with the flow of change and uncertainty, and to accept both the highs and lows that life brings.

The Four Brahmaviharas in Yoga Practice

How do these four brahmaviharas connect to yoga practice? The good news is that we can apply them literally, figuratively, and also as a koan or a riddle. The bad news is that we have to be in relationship with other people to do this work.

Embodying the brahmaviharas isn't terribly hard when we're away on retreat or on vacation, but in our everyday life, we have to practice, fail, make adjustments, and repeat. In the end, it's no different than any other goal. We just help each other muddle along and celebrate the wins when we get them.

Practice & Reflect

Journal:

- Which of the four brahmaviharas comes easily to you?
- Which one are you most likely to struggle with?

Equanimity Reprised

*When you consciously choose to be ordinary,
you become extraordinary.*
— Jaggi Vasudev

Those who feel called to a deeper and more meaningful life frequently have a sense that something is missing. And all of us, at some point or another, have wondered how to fill that sense of unease, or ennui, or meaninglessness. Many paths are available to us, and most of us will have been down several. We'd be pretty boring if we were all on the same one and all wanted the same things.

Equanimity might be described as the ability to let go of path-seeking altogether, or at least the ability to let go of expecting things to be different than they are. But it's not the same thing as nihilism or cynicism. We're not giving up our aspirations, but rather becoming more true to our deep uniqueness, more true to our intuitive, ancient, and wise inner-knowing.

Equanimity is not easy, however, because we're constantly being told that we need to be doing something different or loving something else. We're told we must seize the day and consume all that our heart desires. And that's a thread of being that most of us need to explore to comprehend. I believe there's always going to be a space in our lives that's enhanced by chocolate and ice cream. The drive to pleasure is not the only drive, or the best one, but it's deeply wired and important to survival.

Most of us are experiential learners. People can tell us things, but we don't believe. We learn by making mistakes and failing, and then trying again.

It's difficult for us to imagine a self that isn't moving from A to B on our hypothetical storyline. We think narratively, linearly, and in terms of time passing. We think there's a more perfected self waiting over the horizon, and if anything, that we'd better hurry up and get there. In some of the palliative care trainings I've done, we were asked to imagine that we only have six months to live: What would we do?

I'm not averse to that thought experiment. Country singer Tim McGraw wrote a song on that theme, where the protagonist goes sky-diving, Rocky Mountain climbing, and bull-riding, reads the Bible, becomes more dedicated as a husband and friend, and so on. But the first three activities are just more consumption, which assumes his previous life was inadequate, because he thought he had lots of time so wasn't consuming fast enough. Peak experiences are exciting and bring us into the moment, but as meditators and yogis know, there are much cheaper and easier ways to get there. A similar thought experiment asks you what you would like people to say about you at your funeral. As an aspirational exercise, you could write the eulogy you'd like to have and then do your best to live up to it.

We have a deeply conditioned aversion to being mortal, and riding the swells of joy and pain as they come and go. We have an expectation that we can control the outcomes of our time on the earth, and when it turns out that our power has limits, we can experience a great deal of pain without realizing that it's largely self-inflicted.

Equanimity is the recognition that joy and pain are built in, and the feeling that we're missing something is as natural as having two eyes and a nose. We all feel it, usually when things get quiet. Those who have money and leisure are more likely to suffer from it than those who do not, which is surprising. One need only look at the subset of billionaires who are obsessed with making more money; there's not enough money in all of creation to fill the holes in their souls. But buying and acquiring things is the path they've chosen, and they can circle their way down into that pit-mine until the day they die. Basic needs such as housing, food, safety, and health must be met before any person can exercise much choice or freedom. Beyond that, we don't need much.

The ability to soothe ourselves, to be able to make space for the hard stuff and the parts of us that are sad, lonely, and vulnerable is a cornerstone of equanimity. When we get comfortable with the idea that everything is changing, and there's nothing we can do to make time turn back, we become free. The bad news is that we're in free fall; the good news is that there is no ground. We can accept that we don't have to be happy all the time, and also, that much of our unhappiness is rooted in our own mental preoccupations and habits. We can choose not to be miserable.

Equanimity requires an acceptance of our mortality, our ordinariness, and our smallness. We're here for a very short time. We're exceedingly important to ourselves and those we love, and not important at all in the vastness of time and space. Our actions matter, because we're interconnected and because we have free will, but other than that, individually we're pretty insignificant. Some of us will change the course of history, but not because we planned it. Exceptional people, like Nelson Mandela or Mother Teresa or Bill Gates, didn't have "become famous influencer" on their to-do lists. Their service and invention is what made them important; their influence was a by-product rather than a goal.

Having equanimity means that we don't have to cling to a particular story or religious belief. We're willing to go with whatever happens. If God turns out to be a woman, or a space alien, or a blue whale, we'll still know we lived the best life that we could. We'll accept that we can't know much for sure, and everything is always changing.

Collectively, we can destroy the whole planet trying to make ourselves feel permanent, or we can accept our transience and love one another from day to day—knowing that it's these filaments of love that are holding us together, and really the only thing worth striving for.

Practice & Reflect

Journal:

- If you were to receive a terminal diagnosis tomorrow, what would your priorities be?
- What would you want to do that you're not currently doing?

Wonder and the Source

The true source is pure and stainless.
The branch streams flow in the dark.
— The Sandokai

Equanimity might be thought of as an appreciation of both light and dark, what is known and unknown, the everyday and the astonishing. Our cognitive habits and the necessities of our lives (like holding down a job, making food, cleaning the toilet), can lead us to compare, categorize, and complain. But something else in us, something child-like, imaginative, and untamed, can and does lead us in the opposite direction—toward the ineffable, the sublime, the astonishing—toward wonder.

The word *wonder* has two meanings: as a noun it means something that is marvelous, miraculous, or astonishing. Something that stuns us. As a verb *wonder* means to be curious, uncertain, or intrigued. We all have the capacity to invite and evoke wonder, but most often the path to wonderland does not traverse the thinking, rational part of the brain.

Whether you're religious or an atheist, an artist or a scientist, we all share a sense of wonder about the great mysteries: How did we get here? What happens when we die? Are we alone in the universe, or are there other planets with human-like inhabitants? What is the source of our life? And lest you think these questions don't matter, we've been killing each other over differences in our belief systems for millennia.

We all have some sort of relationship with the source, or God, or if you prefer the language of *Star Wars*, the Force. We love to think about the world having truths and reliable laws to which things conform, like gravity, physics, or more fragile human-made concepts like law and order. We might dismiss the idea of a source altogether (that's also a relationship) or struggle to grasp it through art, drugs, religious rituals, or sensory deprivation tanks. We are experiencers of intuitions, visitations, and visions. But if the mind can conceive of it, if we think we've grasped it, most likely, we've missed it. Grasping it means reducing it, like killing a butterfly and pinning it to a display—we capture the physical aspect of it, but not the essence.

Last year I picked up a bunch of DVDs about astrophysics from the giveaway bin at the local library. And I've been really taken with how religious they are, how rooted in wonder and the intersection of thing and no-thing.

The astrophysicist is working on scales of time in the billions of years. She's using intuition and deductive reasoning. Often a physicist's guesswork turns out to be true: our ability to measure things like the bending of light or gravitational waves lagged far behind our ability to theorize them. We can know things without being able to prove them. But the difference between astrophysicists and religious zealots is that the first works from a position of questioning, and the latter from a position of being right.

Given that we're in the midst of a growing climate emergency, as well as all the violence, racism, misogyny, and more that we've always struggled with through history, I often wonder how much longer the human race can continue. I've found watching the astronomy videos oddly comforting. That we exist at all is a miracle: so many unique conditions had to come together on this planet to keep us from being obliterated. We probably wouldn't be here if we didn't have a huge magnetic field, or if we didn't have the moon, or if we were a little bit closer to or a little bit farther from the sun. The factors at play—the atoms, particles, forces, interplanetary relationships—the sheer size and wonder of it all, they exist. But knowing that doesn't help us to live our lives from day to day.

Looking at the earth from the perspective of deep time helps me to cling a little less. We've been wiped out by asteroid strikes more than once, and yet the planet recovered. I recently learned that whales were once land animals called pakiceti, and that their closest living relatives are hippopotami. So amazing and wondrous things will continue to happen, even if the human species is just too deeply flawed to survive. We can become extinct, and the life source will go on as usual.

We're all made of stardust. We're an integral part of the universe and the big unknowable "mind." We just happen to have a species-wide cognitive limitation. Our minds have allowed us to thrive, make art, build skyscrapers and spaceships, but they obscure the big picture, interdependence, and deep time. We keep looking for a source that is other than or elsewhere, when it's already, and always has been, fully here. On the rare occasions when we can release the fetters of our habits and routines, a deep inner knowing says, "Yes!"

But when we go seeking, that's when things fall apart for us. It's like going on a vacation where everything is brilliant and amazing. The food is delicious, and the sights awe-inspiring. But when we go back to recapture the experience the following year, the staff have changed, there are cockroaches in the bathroom, and the bartender we thought was delightful turns out to be an insufferable narcissist. As soon as we grasp, we're bound for disappointment.

So instead, if we can just stop, and rest in the place between receiving and acting, we can clear out some space for wonder and the unknown. We create conditions where the door can open from the other side, and we can appreciate and take joy in whatever arises. If you have a religious faith or narrative that comforts you, by all means hold it. But it would make the world infinitely more peaceful if we could all make space for others to believe what they believe, space for something new to be born. As things are now, I think a new savior among us is more likely to be murdered or put in prison than to be listened to. We're a species deeply averse to change.

Getting in touch with the source is like sleeping. When we're in deep sleep, our sense of personhood is not present, but deep sleep has an effect. We wake up feeling fresh and renewed. When we don't achieve deep sleep, we feel irritable and unfocused. But we can't grasp what deep sleep is as an experience, because by definition we're unconscious—we can only feel its effects. We know when it's happened by the way we feel. But we can't just turn it on and off. We can't clutch it.

Rather than thinking of the source as a matter of faith, imagine it's a matter of trust. The most basic of practices—sitting still, feeling breath, appreciating the natural world—are among the best techniques we have for experiencing wonder. We don't necessarily need to understand the source or why it works. We do know that it calms us, rejuvenates us, and replenishes our energy. We can get to that place without climbing Everest or traveling to the ends of the earth. The capacity is available and built into us, like the grain of sand that becomes a pearl within the body of an oyster.

Searching for answers, seeking out peak experiences, curiosity, and storytelling are built into our DNA. There's nothing wrong with them, as long as we're in the driver's seat and not the other way around. We could consider them a species-wide habit. Shunryu Suzuki explains, "You are just seeking for something you can understand. That is a mistake."[12] But it's a mistake that's built into our human nature, as are our preferences for good food and a dry place to sleep. We don't need to eliminate the seeker within, but we can stop letting it wear us out. We can recognize it as a friend and traveling companion rather than a master. We can enjoy it and hold it with a sense of lightness, as Dōgen did when he described the life of a Zen master as "one continuous mistake."[13]

We don't really need to know where we're going, or to have a ten-year plan, or the perfect health and fitness regimen. Shunryu Suzuki said, "There is no bird who flies knowing the limit of the sky. There is no fish who swims knowing the end of the ocean."[14] All of the seeking, planning, and goal-setting is completely optional. We can ease up on ourselves, slow down, and rest. We have lots of important things to do, but we'd do them more skillfully and probably more quickly if we stopped striving so hard and tuned in to simplicity, gratitude, and wonder.

Practice & Reflect

Journal:

- What do you wonder about?
- What phenomena allow you to experience wonder?

Friendship

We can count on so few people to go that hard way with us.
— Adrienne Rich

In the children's story *The Velveteen Rabbit*, a forgotten stuffed bunny struggles to fit into the nursery, and to find his place in the hierarchy of relationships. An old Skin Horse explains to him that to become Real, to find the acceptance he's craving, he has to be loved. Never having experienced love, the rabbit asks if it hurts, and the horse replies, "Sometimes ... When you are Real you don't mind being hurt." And then the rabbit asks whether the process happens all at once, or bit by bit. The Skin Horse answers:

> It doesn't happen all at once ... You become. It takes a long time ... Generally by the time you are Real, most of your hair has been loved off, and your eyes drop out and you get loose in the joints and very shabby. But these things don't matter at all, because once you are Real you can't be ugly, except to people who don't understand ... Once you are Real you can't become unreal again. It lasts for always.[15]

We have many ways of talking about love, and when we hear the word "relationship," we default to thinking about sexual unions or familial bonds. But we all have families of birth and also families of choice, the latter made up of our friends.

It's helpful to think about friendship as a practice—something we work at and exercise to get better at. There will be people in our lives for whom we feel an instinctive affinity. It may come down to the fact that they are similar to us. But the friendships that really open us up and transform us are with people who are not at all like us, but who, because of circumstances, we get to know and love.

Harry Potter had Hermione and Ron, Robin Hood had his Merry Men, and Snow White had her Seven Dwarfs. As humans we are wired to need other people. That's why shunning is used as a punishment. From the standpoint of survival, being isolated is a death sentence.

Our friends can reveal the gap between our ideals and our reality, between who we think we are and the choices we routinely make. When we learn a new skill or a new idea, we take it into our relationships to practice. Our friends reflect us back to ourselves, letting us know our good qualities, as well as our not-so-endearing ones—if we hang around long enough. Friendships come to us, as the saying goes, for a reason, a season, or a lifetime. As we all eventually die, our relationships can't last, or at least not in this realm. Entering into a friendship requires a willingness to risk, and a willingness to lose or to be hurt. Fortunately, the benefits almost always outweigh the risks.

Being in relationships changes us. There's an alchemy involved, particularly as friendships grow deeper and longer. Sometimes friendships don't survive for reasons that range from simple incompatibility, to address changes, to death or insurmountable disagreements. Sometimes we have to walk away from friendships when they become damaging or dangerous. Relationships are the arena where we figure out what's safe to share and what's not; what's acceptable and what's not. We also have to learn where our boundaries begin and end, or how much we are willing to give and to take, which is not as simple as you'd think.

In our skull-sized kingdoms (a term owed to David Foster Wallace[16]), we play host to a constant monologue, voiced by an interior narrator who speaks with a sense of authority. She is constantly weighing, measuring, and judging. As we meet other people in the world, she takes them in through the senses and composes stories about them. She creates puppets, character sketches, and facsimiles of the real. She revels in a sense of ownership. *I know* this person, she says. But then, when the puppet-person, the projection, behaves in a way that she doesn't predict, she is shocked and disappointed. How many of us have fallen madly in friendship with a new person, only to discover a year later that they can't "see" us or accept us for who we are?

We are all strangers to one another, even when we think we know each other well. Intimacy takes time, courage, an open mind, and a willingness to participate in a world where we can accept not knowing—*never fully knowing*. Because the other thing that happens is that we are all constantly changing. When we create mind-puppets in place of real people, we don't allow them much flexibility. We don't like it when the characters in our personal soap opera behave in ways that are unpredictable, or that conflict with the me-centered plot we expect to unfurl.

Friendship should be a verb rather than a noun, because if friendships are going to last, they require effort, flexibility, and a willingness to forgive. The more we open ourselves to each other, the more likely we are to be wounded. The mistakes are inevitable—but it's our willingness to try again that determines whether our bonds languish or thrive.

Friendships help us to grow, sometimes in ways that are difficult. According to the Pali Canon (the compiled teachings of the Buddha), when the Buddha was on his death bed, his cousin, friend, and attendant Ananda was overcome with grief. Recognizing that their time together was coming to its end, Ananda asked the Buddha, "Is friendship the most important part of the practice?"

And the Buddha replied, "It's the whole practice."

So when we're obsessed with the form of our practice, or doing things right, or achieving or accomplishing things, it's helpful to remember that practice itself isn't the goal. It's not the destination that's important, but rather the people we meet and the relationships we have along the way. We share our suffering and we share our joy, and the journey is always richer, the luggage lighter, when we travel the road together.

May you walk well, and surrounded by friends.

Practice & Reflect

Journal:

- Write down the names of your closest friend or friends.
- Choose one of these names, and make a short list of the qualities you most appreciate about them.
- Drop that person a note or get in touch to let them know how important they are to you.

Awakened and Free

May you awaken to the mystery of being here and enter the quiet immensity of your own presence.
— John O'Donohue

The ability to stay calm amid chaos is the harvest of a series of spiritual developmental tasks. We're not born with equanimity (unless we're cats), but we do have an innate drive toward wisdom and growth, especially if we have the opportunity to listen to the whispers of our longings.

Caring for our selves, and stepping up to the challenge of daily life with the fullness of our true abilities can be a radical choice. The span of a human life is short: we can do more important things than obsessing about our looks, our weight, or our social media feeds. As we let go of our ideas of self, ironically we become much bigger. Letting go of stories about me versus them, or me versus the world, means that fear stops being our driver, and love has room to come in.

Enough already.

You are enough—good enough, strong enough, wise enough. And chances are that you also have enough stuff.

We've covered seven steps toward reclaiming our sovereignty, the immensity that O'Donohue speaks of. We've taken back our attention and rebuilt our ability to focus using the tools of yoga and mindfulness. We've become curious about our habits, and learned how to tease out our true desires by developing insight about the stories imposed on us by social and economic power structures. We've explored what we stand for and some ethical principles, so that we can feel the solid ground of clarity beneath our decision-making. From discipline and clarity come joy and relaxation.

The work of mindfulness and investigation might feel like an effort, but it's similar to cleaning out the house—there's energy involved, but when it's done, everything feels better. Finally, equanimity is the ability and willingness to find a middle path, and a mature appreciation for contradiction, paradox, and the inevitable ups and downs of being a human adult. With equanimity comes flexibility, humility, and often a sense of humor.

This "enlightened" spiritual maturity is desperately needed, now more than ever. We are at an ecological crisis point, where the survival of the human species may be decided by the choices we make in the next ten years. We're also emerging from a pandemic into world-wide economic uncertainty. Yet it's also a time of great opportunity.

We can be creative, collaborative, and determined. We already have most of the technology we need to turn things around. Collectively we could reimagine the way that we've been living. We could rein in our consumption and choose a lifestyle that includes conservation and reverence for the planet. We can choose to put our health and our relationships front and center, so that we're no longer driven by stress and habit, but rather by love and creativity. We have the power and the ability to change.

I hope this book gives you tools, comfort, and food for thought. May you feel freer to grow in your wisdom and compassion. And whenever you have the chance, choose joy.

Notes

Part One: Concentration

1. Try this breath-counting tip. Look at the fingers on one of your hands (excluding your thumb), and you'll see you have twelve segments. If you touch your thumb to each segment in succession—one segment as you complete each breath—you have a handy-dandy (pun intended) method for keeping track.

2. Nischala Joy Devi, *The Secret Power of Yoga: A Woman's Guide to the Heart and Spirit of the Yoga Sutras* (New York: Three Rivers Press, 2007), 253.

3. B.K.S. Iyengar, *Light on Pranayama: The Definitive Guide to the Art of Breathing* (London: Thorsons, 2013), 257.

4. Note from Matt Remski's "Meditation Remixed," course on Mettaversity, accessed November 11, 2016, https://mettaversity.com/meditation-yoga-online-course.

5. David Frawley, *Yoga and Ayurveda: Self-Healing and Self-Realization* (Wisconsin: Lotus Press, 1999), 261–272.

6. The "Six Openings Seal," or Shanmukhi Mudra, uses the fingers or props to close the eyes, plug the ears, and close the nostrils. The goal is to quiet the sense organs by blocking them.

7. There is a pose named after the tortoise, called Kurmasana. I haven't included instructions, because to accomplish it safely you have to be exceptionally flexible.

8. Ravi Chandra, "How to Use Social Media Wisely and Mindfully," mindful.org (January 23, 2018), Accessed February 21, 2018, https://www.mindful.org/use-social-media-wisely-mindfully.

9. Chandra, "How to Use Social Media."

10. John Bell and John Zada, "The Great Attention Heist," *LA Review of Books* (January 1, 2018), accessed February 21, 2018, https://lareviewofbooks.org/article/the-great-attention-heist/#1.

11. Chandra, "How to Use Social Media."

12. Leila Mead, "2019 Earth Overshoot Day Reaches Earliest Date Ever," IISG SDG Knowledge Hub (August 1, 2019), accessed November 19, 2019, https://sdg.iisd.org/news/2019-earth-overshoot-day-reaches-earliest-date-ever.

13. Mead, "2019 Earth Overshoot Day."

Part Two: Mindfulness

1. Dr. Willoughby Britton, PhD, "Adverse Effects in Meditation Practice," podcast audio, *Awake in the World Podcast* (November 2013), accessed February 28, 2020, https://tinyurl.com/yy4z2k4v.

2. Richard Freeman, *The Mirror of Yoga: Awakening the Intelligence of Body and Mind* (Boston: Shambhala, 2012), 167–168.

Part Three: Investigation

1. Craig Hase and Devon Hase, *How Not to Be a Hot Mess: A Survival Guide for Modern Life* (Boston: Shambhala, 2020), excerpted in *Tricycle: The Buddhist Review* (Spring 2020) :37.

2. Rumi, *The Essential Rumi*, trans. Coleman Barks (New York: HarperOne, 2004), 13. My friend Grant sent this poem, perfect for this pandemic, to our sangha: "There is no need to go outside . . ." It moved me.

3. *Ego* is a Latin word Sigmund Freud adopted to describe the mental mediator between the biological/unconscious drives we're born with, and the need to cooperate and manage relationships with others.

4. Chip Hartranft, *The Yoga-Sutra of Patanjali* (Boston: Shambhala, 2003), 106.

5. Jonathan Chabout, Abhra Sarkar, David B. Dunson, and Erich D. Jarvis, "Male Mice Song Syntax Depends on Social Contexts and Influences Female Preferences," *Frontiers in Behavioral Neuroscience* (April 1, 2015), accessed December 9, 2019, DOI: 10.3389/fnbeh.2015.00076.

6. Richard Freeman, *The Mirror of Yoga: Awakening the Intelligence of Body and Mind* (Boston: Shambhala, 2012), 82.

7. Thomas King, *The Inconvenient Indian: A Curious Account of Native People in North America* (Toronto: Anchor Canada, 2013).

8. Ursula K. Le Guin, *The Wave in the Mind: Talks and Essays on the Writer, the Reader, and the Imagination* (Boston: Shambhala, 2004), 218.

9. "The Fourteen Mindfulness Trainings," plumvillage.org (February 2012), accessed September 26, 2018, https://plumvillage.org/mindfulness-practice/the-14-mindfulness-trainings.

Part Four: Virya

1. The Mahabharata is one of the great Hindu texts and includes within its pages the Bhagavad Gita. Virabhadra the warrior appears there as a fierce avatar of the Hindu god, Shiva (the Destroyer).

2. These stages, and several more, are eloquently described in the essay "The Eight Stages of Monastic Practice" by Norman Fisher, available at http://www.whiterobedmonks.org/mstages.html.

3. Andrew Olendzki, "What's in a Word? Karma," *Tricycle: The Buddhist Review* (Fall 2019), 42.

4. Richard Freeman, *The Mirror of Yoga: Awakening the Intelligence of Body and Mind* (Boston: Shambhala, 2012), 200.

5. Marie Scarles, "Finding Freedom Right Here, Right Now, An Interview with Jack Kornfield," *Tricycle: The Buddhist Review* (May 8, 2017).

6. Alison Snowden and David Fine, "Animal Behaviour," animated short, 14 min., 2018, accessed https://www.nfb.ca/film/animal_behaviour.

7. Damian Carrington, "Humanity Has Wiped Out 60% of Animal Populations Since 1970, Report Finds," TheGuardian.com (October 30, 2018), accessed August 22, 2019, https://www.theguardian.com/environment/2018/oct/30/humanity-wiped-out-animals-since-1970-major-report-finds.

8. Richard Freeman. *The Mirror of Yoga* (Boston: Shambhala, 2012), 35.

9. Edward Brown, "The Vision Cow: Edward Espe Brown Adapts the Traditional Zen Ox-Herding Series," *Tricycle: The Buddhist Review* (Spring 2001), accessed September 8, 2016, https://tinyurl.com/y24wbbso.

10. The history of sexuality is a massive topic and the subject of many books and academic theses, so I am vastly condensing and oversimplifying here. Early Christian thinkers portrayed women as non-sexual beings who behaved as temptresses for other reasons, mainly leading to the downfall of men. Philosophers at the time understood that sex between a man and a woman led to conception, but they believed that the woman donated the physical body and the man was responsible for the soul and the intellect, i.e., the immortal part.

11. Michel Foucault, "Nietzsche, Genealogy, History," in *The Foucault Reader*, ed. Paul Rabinow (New York: Pantheon, 1984), 87.

12. Michel Foucault, "The Subject and Power," in *Michel Foucault: Beyond Structuralism and Hermeneutics*, eds. Hubert L. Dreyfus and Paul Rabinow (Chicago: University of Chicago Press, 1982), 208–226.

13. Marie Christine Leps, "Critical Production of Discourse: Angenot, Bahktin, Foucault," *The Yale Journal of Criticism* 17.2 (2004): 279.

14. On November 13, 2015, three suicide bombers detonated explosives at a football match in Saint-Denis, a north Paris suburb, and gunmen carried out a mass shooting at a concert at the Bataclan Theatre in Paris. Several smaller attacks were perpetrated at a number of sidewalk cafés and restaurants. In all, 130 people were killed and another 413 injured. The terrorist group Islamic State of Iraq and the Levant (ISIL) claimed responsibility and said the attacks were in retaliation for French airstrikes on ISIL in Syria and Iraq.

15. David Emery, "Did MLK Say 'Our Lives Begin to End the Day We Become Silent'?" snopes.com, January 16, 2017, accessed May 30, 2020, https://www.snopes.com/fact-check/mlk-our-lives-begin-to-end.

16. Martin Luther King, Jr., Quotes, *BrainyQuote.com*, BrainyMedia Inc, 2020, accessed June 2, 2020, https://www.brainyquote.com/quotes/martin_luther_king_jr_103571.

Part Five: Joy

1. "Exploring the Powerful Emotion of Awe: How It Can Be Awe-some and Awe-ful," *Quirks & Quarks*, CBC radio show, 19:27, originally aired March 19, 2019, accessed August 27, 2019, https://www.cbc.ca/radio/quirks/exploring-the-powerful-emotion-of-awe-how-it-can-be-awe-some-and-aw-ful-1.5047156.

2. Emily Vey Duke and Cooper Battersby are visual and film artists. For more information and a sampling of their work, see http://dukeandbattersby.com/wp/about.

3. Anthropomorphizing is the tendency to project human traits and emotions onto animals.

Part Six: Relaxation

1. I am aware this essay has a built-in assumption of privilege. Many people who live in poverty or uncertainty or who lack the most basic needs like shelter and safety may not have the luxury of leisure or relaxation.

2. Pema Chödrön, *The Places that Scare You: A Guide to Fearlessness in Difficult Times* (Boston: Shambhala, 2002), 11–15.

3. "Earth Peace Treaty Commitment Sheet," accessed March 12, 2016, https://earthholder.training/earth-loving-practices-for-simple-ethical-living.

4. Rolf Sovik is an American yoga teacher, and president and spiritual director of the Himalayan Institute. This model of the respiratory system was a component of a course he taught through Yoga International: https://yogainternational.com/profile/rolf-sovik#more.

5. "Wabi-sabi," Wikipedia, accessed May 28, 2020, https://en.wikipedia.org/wiki/Wabi-sabi.

Part Seven: Equanimity

1. Daisy Hernández, "The Noble Abode of Equanimity," *Tricycle: The Buddhist Review*, 28, no. 4 (Summer 2019), 56–59, 100–101.

2. James Baldwin, *Notes of a Native Son* (Boston: Beacon Press, 1955, 1984), 113.

3. Zen Peacemakers International, "Our Story," accessed August 31, 2019, https://zenpeacemakers.org/our-story.

4. Alan Cross, "David Bowie Dead of Cancer at Age 69," *A Journal of Musical Things* (January 12, 2016), accessed January 18, 2016, https://www.ajournalofmusicalthings.com/david-bowie-dead-of-cancer-at-age-69.

5. Chip Hartranft, *The Yoga-Sutra of Patanjali* (Boston: Shambhala, 2003), 101.

6. David Reich Chadwick, "Suzuki and Other Quotes from Crooked Cucumber, sent by FF Miller, 2016," *Cuke.com*, accessed August 31, 2019, http://www.cuke.com/Crooked%20Cucumber/cc%20excerpts/cc-quotes-miller.htm.

7. Jessica Lamb-Shapiro, *Promise Land: My Journey Through America's Self-Help Culture* (Toronto: Simon and Schuster, 2014), 206.

8. Jack Kornfield, *After the Ecstasy, the Laundry: How the Heart Grows Wise on the Spiritual Path* (New York: Bantam Books, 2000), 82.

9. Laura Entis, "Read Sheryl Sandberg's Poignant Facebook Post on Losing Her Husband," www.entrepreneur.com (June 3, 2015), accessed November 8, 2016, https://www.entrepreneur.com/article/246943.

10. A digression: I've come across a perfume called Samsara, as well as a health spa and a chain of retirement homes. (You probably want to give that retirement home a miss.)

11. Acknowledgment is due here to Pema Chödrön, who explains these four qualities in terms of "near enemies" and "far enemies." Although I have changed the wording, the conceptual framework is hers. See: Chödrön, Pema, *The Places that Scare You: A Guide to Fearlessness in Difficult Times* (Boston: Shambhala, 2002), 27.

12. Shunryu Suzuki, *Branching Streams Flow in the Darkness: Zen Talks on the Sandokai,* eds. Mel Weitsman and Michael Wenger (Berkeley: University of California Press), 58–59.

13. Suzuki, *Branching Streams*, 59.

14. The quote is attributed to Dōgen, but this exact wording does not appear in any of his translated writings. It seems to be a condensation of a longer quote from Dōgen's Genjo-Koan, summed up by Shunryu Suzuki.

15. Margery Williams, *The Velveteen Rabbit* (New York: Doubleday, 1922), 5–8.

16. David Foster Wallace, *This Is Water: Some Thoughts Delivered on a Significant Occasion, about Living a Compassionate Life* (New York: Little, Brown and Company, 2009), 117.

Glossary

Abhinivesa: fear of death, fear of letting go of the story of "me," self-preservation.

Ahamkara: the part of our consciousness that fabricates our identity; sometimes called "the I-maker."

Ahimsa: the ethical principle (yama) of not doing harm, or, conversely, recognizing that we are all interdependent and not "separate."

Anatta: the Buddhist principle of "non-self," which stipulates that what feels like a "self" is really the juxtaposition of memories, conditions, language, and moments in time. In this light the self is real, but constantly evolving and changing.

Antara Yoga (also called Samyama): the journey from the "everyday" world to the interior world of consciousness and enlightenment; the discipline that leads to liberation and release from suffering.

Aparigraha: the ethical principle of not grasping or being greedy, or, conversely, being content.

Asteya: the ethical principle of not stealing, or not taking anything that is not offered freely. The flip side is the cultivation of generosity.

Avidya: the inability to see things as they really are; delusion.

Bodhicitta: the impulse to grow; the drive toward awakening.

Brahmacharya: the ethical principle of restraint in the realm of sexuality.

Brahmaviharas: the four aspirational behaviors embodied by the wise: Metta, Maitri, Mudita, and Upekkha.

Dakinis: female deities ("sky-dancers") who embody the positive energy of anger but are free of aggression or hatred. They transform anger into skillful action.

Dharana: the ability to keep the attention on a singular focus for short periods.

Dhyana: meditation; the ability to keep the attention on a singular focus for a sustained period.

Dukkha: the natural state of dissatisfaction or suffering that is part of the human experience.

Gaki: "hungry ghosts," a Buddhist metaphor for the part of us that can never be satisfied.

Gunas: the three threads or strands of energy that make up all of matter and include sattva, rajas, and tamas; the qualities of nature.

Hatha Yoga: the form of yoga that developed following the decline of Buddhism in India and described in the *Hatha Yoga Pradipika* as well as other texts. This is also an umbrella term used for almost all forms of modern postural practice.

Interbeing/Interdependence: the Buddhist principle that views all components of the universe as completely intertwined with all other forms.

Ishvara Pranidana: surrender to a higher power or god; a recognition that some things are beyond our control.

Karma: the actions we take and the outcomes that are produced because of them.

Kriya Yoga: the "yoga of action," which consists of tapas, svadyaya, and ishvara pranidana.

Maitri: compassion toward the self and for others.

Metta: the Buddhist term for loving-kindness.

Mudita: taking joy in the happiness of others.

Niyamas: the ethical guidelines that relate to how we take care of ourselves—including sauca, santosha, tapas, svadyaya, and ishvara pranidana.

Patanjali's Yoga Sutras: a compilation of 196 aphorisms written about 200 C.E. to describe and summarize the broad variety of teachings that made up yoga. Heavily influenced by Buddhism, the practices outlined in the yoga sutras are sometimes described as "classical" or "raja" yoga.

Pranayama: techniques that alter breathing patterns and affect the movement of energy (and the nervous system).

Pratyahara: withdrawal of attention from the external world to the internal one.

Samsara: the cycle of life; the "wheel" of birth and death; existence in the material world.

Samskara: the repetition of habit patterns and behaviors.

Santosha: contentment.

Sati/Smrti: Pali/Sanskrit terms for mindfulness. From the root *smr*, "to remember." Present-focused attention that is non-judgmental, steady, intentional, and gentle.

Samadhi: integration, union, the dropping away of self, oneness, absorption.

Samyama (also called Antara Yoga): the journey from the external, material world toward samadhi.

Satya: the ethic (yama) of honesty or truth.

Sauca: purity and cleanliness (one of the niyamas).

Shamata: the calm, concentrated state developed through mindfulness practice.

Shikantaza: a Zen term meaning "just sitting." An open-awareness style of meditation that does not require focus on a particular object.

Shiva: one of the main deities of Hinduism, Shiva is the representative of death and destruction (in the service of rebirth), of meditation and pure awareness, and of yogis and asceticism.

Svadyaya: self-study, in the sense of both introspection and self-directed learning.

Tapas: intensity, heat, fire, effort.

Vipassana: a meditative technique, and also "insight."

Virya: energy, enthusiasm, vigor, courage.

Wabi-sabi: an esthetic principle that celebrates transience and imperfection.

Yamas: the five ethical principles relating to conduct in relationships with others.

Recommended Reading

Chödrön, Pema. *The Places that Scare You: A Guide to Fearlessness in Difficult Times*. Boston: Shambhala, 2002. I recommend everything Pema Chödrön has written, and she's written extensively.

Devi, Nischala Joy. *The Secret Power of Yoga: A Woman's Guide to the Heart and Spirit of the Yoga Sutras*. New York: Three Rivers Press, 2007.

Duhigg, Charles. *The Power of Habit: Why We Do What We Do in Life and Business*. New York: Random House, 2014.

Forleo, Marie. *Everything Is Figureoutable*. New York: Penguin, 2019.

Foster Wallace, David. *This Is Water: Some Thoughts Delivered on a Significant Occasion, about Living a Compassionate Life*. New York: Little, Brown and Company, 2009.

Freeman, Richard. *The Mirror of Yoga: Awakening the Intelligence of Body and Mind*. Boston: Shambhala, 2012.

Gilbert, Daniel. *Stumbling on Happiness*. Toronto: Vintage Canada, 2006.

Hartranft, Chip. *The Yoga-Sutra of Patanjali*. Boston: Shambhala, 2003.

Kendi, Ibram X. *How to Be an Antiracist*. New York: One World, 2019.

Nichtern, Ethan. *The Dharma of the Princess Bride*. New York: North Point Press, 2017.

O'Donohue, John. *Eternal Echoes: Celtic Reflections on Our Yearning to Belong*. New York: Perennial, 1999.

Stone, Michael. *The Inner Tradition of Yoga: A Guide to Yoga Philosophy for the Contemporary Practitioner*. Boston: Shambhala, 2008.

Stone, Michael. *The World Comes to You: Notes on Practice, Love, and Social Action*, edited by Erin Robinsong. Boulder: Shambhala, 2019.

Stone, Michael. *Yoga for a World Out of Balance: Teachings on Ethics and Social Action*. Boston: Shambhala, 2009.

Suzuki, Shunryu. *Zen Mind, Beginner's Mind: Informal Talks on Zen Meditation and Practice.* Boston: Shambhala, 2011.

Thich Nhat Hahn. *Peace Is Every Step: The Path of Mindfulness in Everyday Life*, edited by Arnold Kotler. Toronto: Bantam Books. 1991.

Acknowledgments

The teachings within this book are distilled from the texts, traditions and yoga/dharma teachers of India, Afghanistan, China, Japan, Thailand and elsewhere in Asia. Those of us who study Yoga and Buddhism owe a debt of gratitude to these great wisdom traditions and the cultures from which they originated, as well as to the many teachers and writers who have been sharing this knowledge for millennia, often without recognition.

Although writing a book can feel like a solitary endeavor, the opposite is true. I am incredibly grateful for the support and assistance of my nearest and dearest friends, who provided encouragement, sounding boards, and gentle prods—particularly at times when I was ready to burn the manuscript and take up knitting.

Special thanks to Jenn Sharko, my assistant and cheerleader, and to Kim McDougall, designer and publisher, who is also a funny and supportive friend. Thanks to Ian James, who volunteered to proof read (even though he's not interested in yoga) and who caught a biblical error. Kudos also to editor extraordinaire, Allyson Latta, who convinced me that I actually was writing a self-help book, and who asked all the right questions with kindness and clarity.

To my support group of beautiful unicorns (Katie, Sue, Tanya, and Vicki), you never fail to amaze me. And thank you to my yoga teachers past and present, in particular Brenda Sharpe, Esther Myers, Paola di Paolo, Monica Voss, Tama Soble, Deb Orr, Jill Miller, and my brilliant friend YuMee Chung, who is a model of dedication to the craft of teaching. Gratitude as well to another teacher of mine, Fides Krucker, who has unveiled a whole new world of breath, voice, and self-expression that came as an utter surprise to me. Special thanks to my colleagues Charlene Biggerstaff, Elan Boyd, Jillian Cook, Lydia Pollock, and Sandy Wickeler, who understand how hard it is to "walk the talk" and who provided friendship when the going was hard.

For friendship and dharma practice, deepest appreciation and bows to the Gravity Toronto Sangha (formerly Centre of Gravity). It is so good to have many wise and kind people to look up to. Also, thank you to my writing group friends (Carly, Carolin, Lauren, Mary Anne, and Sara) and the Writers' Community of York Region, for camaraderie, encouragement, and the 2019 Writer's Grant. For the many times I was ready to give up but didn't, I have to thank Marie Forleo, an upbeat tour de force whom I don't know personally but feel like I do. And of course, I want to acknowledge Michael Stone, who taught me most of the important things I know, and whom I will always carry in my heart. (Michael's teachings are available online at www.michaelstoneteaching.com).

To my students both past and present, who've given me so much joy and laughter through the years, and who are wise and funny in all the best ways—thank you. And deepest gratitude to my blood family and my friend family, who have filled my life with love, adventures, and a lot of really delicious food. You know who you are.

Most of all, thank you to David Pierce, who made the entire project possible, and who secretly built me a tree house to write in. As Hafiz wrote: "A love like that can light up the whole sky." I really do owe it all to you.

Dear Reader,

I know that your time is precious and in short supply, so thank you from the bottom of my heart for taking the time to read this book. It means a lot to me.

I send out occasional updates and blog posts via a newsletter you can subscribe to on my website.

If you've enjoyed this book, please consider leaving a review. In these days of algorithms and automation reviews are critical: they help readers to know what to expect, they let me know how the book has been received, and they help booksellers decide what to show to new readers.

If you would like to leave a review or subscribe to the newsletter, please visit www.jacksonyoga.ca.

Wishing you peace and love,

Elaine Jackson

About the Author

If Elaine had her way, she'd spend most of her time outside, curled up with a book, or sharing picnics with friends. She is a perpetual student, idea-collector, nature-lover, cyclist, cat momma, and explorer. After a long career as an occupational therapist and many years of teaching yoga and meditation, she's fascinated with the power we have to heal ourselves—if only we are aware of it. She lives with her husband in rural Ontario in a house that lacks for nothing except a high-speed internet connection. You can find her online at www.jacksonyoga.ca.

www.ingramcontent.com/pod-product-compliance
Lightning Source LLC
Chambersburg PA
CBHW020903080526
44589CB00011B/423